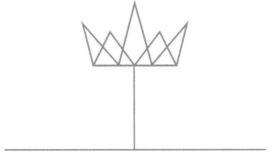

SEEK FIRST
THE
KINGDOM

GOD'S INVITATION
TO LIFE AND JOY IN THE
BOOK OF MATTHEW

CHRISTINE HOOVER

Lifeway Press®
Brentwood, Tennessee

Published by Lifeway Press® • © 2023 Christine Hoover

ISBN: 978-1-0877-8639-1 • Item: 005842592
Dewey decimal classification: 226.2
Subject headings: CHRISTIAN LIFE / KINGDOM OF GOD / BIBLE. N.T. MATTHEW–STUDY AND TEACHING

To order additional copies of this resource, write to Lifeway Church Resources Customer Service; 200 Powell Place, Suite 100, Brentwood, TN 37027-7707; FAX order to 615.251.5933; call toll-free 800.458.2772; email orderentry@lifeway.com; or order online at lifeway.com.

Author is represented by Wolgemuth & Associates, Inc.

Printed in the United States of America

Lifeway Women Bible Studies
Lifeway Resources
200 Powell Place, Suite 100,
Brentwood, TN 37027-7707

Cover design by Lauren Ervin

EDITORIAL TEAM, LIFEWAY WOMEN BIBLE STUDIES

Becky Loyd
Director, Lifeway Women

Tina Boesch
Manager

Sarah Doss
Team Leader

Ivan Mesa
Content Editor

Lindsey Bush
Production Editor

Chelsea Waack
Graphic Designer

TABLE OF CONTENTS

4   ABOUT THE AUTHOR
5   FOREWORD: THE WHYS AND HOWS OF STUDYING MATTHEW
8   AN INTRODUCTION TO THE BOOK OF MATTHEW

10 SESSION ONE: THE KING HAS COME

34 SESSION TWO: ENTERING THE KINGDOM

62 SESSION THREE: THE CULTURE OF THE KINGDOM

90 SESSION FOUR: LIVING THE KINGDOM LIFE

114 SESSION FIVE: EXPANDING THE KINGDOM

140 SESSION SIX: CHARACTERISTICS OF THE KINGDOM

166 SESSION SEVEN: THE COMMUNITY OF THE KINGDOM

192 SESSION EIGHT: THE KINGDOM TO COME

216 LEADER GUIDE
221 ENDNOTES
222 HOW TO BECOME A CHRISTIAN
225 VIDEO REDEMPTION CARD

ABOUT THE AUTHOR

Christine Hoover is a pastor's wife, mom of three boys, host of the *By Faith* podcast, and author of several books, including *With All Your Heart: Living Joyfully Through Allegiance to King Jesus, Searching for Spring, Messy Beautiful Friendship,* and *From Good to Grace.* Her work has appeared on *Christianity Today, The Gospel Coalition,* and *For the Church.* Originally from Texas, Christine and her family live in Charlottesville, Virginia, where they planted a church in 2008. Find her at her home online at ChristineHoover.net.

FOREWORD
THE WHYS AND HOWS OF STUDYING MATTHEW

Welcome to a wonderfully rich book of the Bible—the Book of Matthew. In our study together over the coming weeks, we'll discover who Jesus is, why He is called King, and what it means to be a citizen under His rule and reign in the kingdom of God.

WHY STUDY THE BIBLE?

If, as Scripture says, "Faith comes from hearing, and hearing through the word of Christ" (Rom. 10:17), God fuels and feeds our faith specifically through His Word. This is why we study the Bible. We're renewed and transformed by the Holy Spirit as we present and submit ourselves to His Word. This growth process, however, doesn't happen overnight. Jesus said it happens more similarly to how a seed grows (Mark 4:26-27). The seed is first nestled in the ground, unseen. Then its tender, fragile sprout breaks through the soil. Over time, the plant grows sturdier and taller, roots ever-deepening. After several years, the plant proves its identity as a tree by bearing fruit.

In this analogy, we're neither the seed nor the tree; we're the soil in which the seed is planted. Jesus said that when we receive, study, and embrace the good seed of the Word, He grows a strong, fruit-bearing faith in us. To "hear and understand" (Matt. 15:10) the Word gives a sense of bending toward a speaker, intent on catching every word in order to obey every word. This is why we study the Bible: we're presenting ourselves to God for our daily deposit and "watering" of His truth. The promise Jesus gave us is that by doing so, the Spirit will change us, and He will give us deep refreshment in our inner being.

My prayer for you as you begin this study is that you will be good soil, a ready receptacle for God's Word.

WHY STUDY THE BOOK OF MATTHEW?

Matthew provides the most comprehensive collection of Jesus' teachings in one book, which is reason enough to study it. But one of the book's most significant characteristics is the interchange we can observe between Jesus' words and His actions. He proclaims truth and then models how to live and relate to others according to those truths.

Studying Matthew also helps us understand the kingdom of God, a topic Jesus focused on often. Most of us have heard the phrase "the kingdom of God," but we have little working knowledge of what the kingdom of God is and how it impacts our daily lives. Thankfully, the Book of Matthew tackles the kingdom from multiple angles, helping to locate us in God's story and inviting us to find life with and through Jesus in this kingdom.

The Book of Matthew is ultimately a proclamation to us of who our King is. This King—Jesus—constantly draws our eyes to "look at" what we can't see with physical eyes—a different kingdom from where we currently live. This unseen kingdom, He will repeatedly say to us, is our true home. My prayer for you as you begin this study is that you will have spiritual eyes to see this kingdom God is building through His chosen King: Jesus.

HOW TO STUDY THE BIBLE

Perhaps you are new to Bible study or you lack confidence in your Bible study skills. I'm glad you've chosen this study! The layout of this Bible study book is intended not only to guide your study but also to teach you *how* to study. The structure is based upon questions you can take with you as you study other books of the Bible:

What does the passage say? In other words, what are the facts or truths the author is expressing? Look specifically for the following:

- What does this say about God's character or nature?
- What does this say about God's actions, whether past, present, or future?
- What does this say about people, both in general and in relation to God?
- What does this say about a person's response to God's actions? In other words, what command is to be obeyed?

What does the passage mean? Think about the passage in the larger context of the book and the even larger context of Scripture. Context often helps bring clarity to the author's intended meaning. If there are confusing words or phrases, stop and consider them until you have more clarity. Use tools such as cross references, various versions of the Bible, and a dictionary. These should be used often when studying the Bible.

How must I respond? Allow the Holy Spirit to personalize the text. Is there something to confess and repent of? Something to think about? Something on which to take action? Something in which to rejoice?

My prayer for you as you begin this study is that you would better know the character and nature of King Jesus and would respond with undivided allegiance to Him.

HOW TO USE THIS BIBLE STUDY BOOK

Now that you're ready to dig in, here's a look at where to begin and how to structure your study experience.

START HERE: Each session of *Seek First the Kingdom* begins with a teaching video from Christine. You'll want to start this study by watching the Session One teaching video and reading the Introduction on pages 8–9.

PERSONAL STUDY: Each session also includes five days of personal study. The Wrap-Up pages provide you with a place to take notes from your small group discussion time and the video teachings.

PART OF A GROUP? When you gather, discuss your personal study and watch the next week's teaching video. The leader guide on page 216 offers several tips and helps along with discussion guides for each week.

VIDEO ACCESS: With the purchase of this book, you have access to videos from Christine that provide insight to help you better understand and apply what you study. You'll find detailed information for how to stream the video teaching sessions on the card inserted in the back of this book.

MATTHEW READING PLAN: On a side note, the Book of Matthew is quite long, and your study will not cover every verse, nor will it be studied in the order it's written. In order to "hear and understand" Matthew, I encourage you to read or listen to the entire book several times throughout your study. Listening may be easier, because you can access audio as you drive, exercise, or do mundane work. If you choose to read it, I've provided a reading plan online at **lifeway.com/seekfirst**. Look and listen for themes and recurring phrases. Look and listen for descriptions of Jesus. Finally, look and listen for specific descriptions of the kingdom of God and your place in it.

May God show you the blessing of living under the rule and reign of Jesus.

AN INTRODUCTION TO THE BOOK OF MATTHEW

We live in a world of identity confusion. Who are we? What determines our value? Where do we belong? What is our purpose? And perhaps the most important question: who gets to determine the definitive answers to these questions?

Identity is important because how we define ourselves is ultimately the bedrock of our lives, the foundation on which we build and make decisions about how we'll live. We embrace an identity—a story about ourselves and our place in this world—that we believe will lead to our thriving. In other words, we often find our security in the roles and labels by which we identify. Where we place our identity is where we think we'll find life.

Our world, in search of life, exalts self to the ultimate place. This should not be an affront or a surprise. We come into this world factory set on self, and we'll seek anything that feeds a sense of satisfaction, glory, or security.

Christians are not immune to this same confusion. Although we're in Christ and filled by His Spirit, we continue carrying our flesh with us everywhere we go, and our flesh constantly pulls us toward self-reliance, self-exaltation, and self-justification. We're easily disoriented, quickly losing sight of God and our place in His story.

This is why the Book of Matthew is significant, for both the follower of self and the follower of Jesus. Matthew tells us how God locates, finds, and invites us to find all the life and secure identity we could ever hope for. We'll discover in Matthew that God does this work through Jesus, and we'll find that Jesus came telling a story about a kingdom He called the kingdom of God. The kingdom of God as we'll define it in this study is a *people* who enjoy God's *provision* and rest under His *protective power* in a specific *place*.

You and I are meant for this kingdom, we're identified by this kingdom, and this is good news for us in a world of confusion.

In the Book of Matthew, we'll watch and listen as Jesus proclaims the kingdom. In Matthew 4:23, for example, it says, "And [Jesus] went throughout all Galilee, teaching in their synagogues and proclaiming the gospel of the kingdom and healing every disease and every affliction among the people."

To proclaim means to announce. When a couple in the British royal family has a baby, their tradition is to set out on an easel in front of Buckingham Palace a written announcement outlining the details of the birth. Similarly, Jesus' mission and ministry was to be an embodied announcement from God. This announcement was a proclamation of life.

WATCH THE SESSION ONE VIDEO. To access the video teaching sessions, use the instructions in the back of your Bible study book. You can find group discussion questions in the leader guide on page 216.

The invitation of the kingdom is to find this true life—life as it was intended by God to be. Our search for identity, significance, peace, satisfaction, and purpose is ultimately a search for kingdom life. Jesus, as we'll see in Matthew, says this life is available for those who seek it, and it's a life that will extend beyond physical death. In fact, we continue today waiting for the final fulfillment of this promise of eternal life.

Earlier I listed the questions we all ask in this life: Who am I? What determines my value? Where do I belong? What is my purpose? The most important question, however, was this: who gets to determine the definitive answers to these questions?

The Bible tells us that because Jesus is King, He alone is the One who has the authority to answer our questions. When we become His, Matthew tells us, this is what He says:

Who are we? We're children of God, sustained and provided for.

What determines our value? We rest under the good rule and reign of Jesus.

Where do we belong? We belong to the kingdom of God, a kingdom that will last forever.

What is our purpose? We're to enjoy our King and imitate Him in the world, participating in the cultivation of the kingdom.

It's difficult to be a dependent, peaceful, rejoicing child in a world being torn to shreds, but one of the greatest truths about the kingdom of God is that it gives to us that which it demands. We're not asked to give our allegiance to a disengaged, tyrannical king. We give our allegiance to the King who gives His in return and will never take it away.

The invitation stands. Do you want life? Then you want the King and His kingdom.

I can't wait to lead you on your exploration of the Book of Matthew.

THE *king* HAS COME

SESSION ONE

In 2008, my family and I moved from a small, conservative college town in Texas to a small, liberal college town in Virginia to plant a church. Our new city, we quickly learned, prides itself on intellectualism, progressive politics, and tolerance—a vastly different demographic than from where we'd come. Although he had years of preaching and teaching experience in our previous church, my husband Kyle had to learn new ways of communicating the same ancient truths in hopes of reaching everyone from the intellectual skeptic to the listener with no Bible knowledge. The task was both challenging and exhilarating as we witnessed God matching His truth to our community's context and needs.

Context matters. As we begin our study of Matthew, we must similarly understand the context in which the author (traditionally thought to be Matthew, the tax-collector-turned-disciple) wrote and the audience to whom he wrote. His context and audience often informed his choice of words, and knowing this helps us comprehend his message about who Jesus is and what He came to do.

Matthew wrote his Gospel with a particular audience in mind: Jews just like himself. He repeatedly built a bridge between the Old and New Testament eras, naming prophecies and lineages as proof to a Jewish audience that Jesus is the Messiah. Notably, Matthew most often used "Son of David" as a name for Jesus, a term his Jewish audience would instinctively connote with royalty. The Jews had known for centuries that God would inaugurate an eternal kingdom, and Matthew connected Jesus to the kingly line of David. Matthew made it clear: the kingdom of God was inaugurated in the person and work of Jesus Christ.

Because Matthew bridged the two testaments, in our study this week we'll connect Old Testament promises, patriarchs, and prophecies to the Man Matthew said is the long-awaited Messiah—Jesus Christ. We'll answer questions about where this Man came from, who He is, and what He did two thousand years ago that continues to influence our lives today.

The beginning of Matthew reads much like a newborn's baby book. We discover the details of Jesus' birth, the backstory of His family, and why these details are notable. This is, of course, where we'll begin. But we'll also skip ahead to the very end in order to read about Jesus' death. The baby book and the obituary are the bookends of every person's life. However, what happens after the writing of Jesus' obituary is what proves He is not just any other person. The ending adds weight and significance to everything Jesus said and did, and who He claimed to be—if we accept it—completely rewrites your life and mine, from baby book to the grave.

THE KING'S HERITAGE

People are often fascinated by uncovering their family trees and learning who their ancestors were and where they came from. For someone of royal birth, however, the significance of their lineage goes far beyond fascination or interesting facts: their place in the family tree equates to title and authority. Because of this, a royal lineage is carefully chronicled and kept throughout generations and centuries.

READ MATTHEW 1:1-17.

Matthew began his book with a genealogy. While we're often tempted in our Bible reading to skip genealogies, Matthew begins with one for a significant reason: the author is establishing Jesus' family heritage. Jewish families kept detailed records of their lineage in order to legally establish familial rights and inheritance. Matthew tells us to look at these key people—and the promises given to them—to help frame how we read the entire book and how we understand who Jesus is.[1] His heritage tells a significant story.

1) Matthew establishes Jesus' familial connection to two significant people from Jewish history. Who are they (v. 1)?

• Jesus, the Son of _____

• Jesus, the Son of _____

2) The Book of Luke (3:23-38) lists a different genealogy for Jesus. Luke emphasized the biological descent of Jesus from Adam. By connecting Jesus primarily with Abraham and David, what was Matthew emphasizing in his genealogy?

3) David and Abraham are significant in Jewish history because God made promises to both of them. Much of the Old Testament can be understood according to the "eras" of these men. What promises did God make to them?

- Abraham (at the time called Abram) in Genesis 12:1-3; 15:5-7:

- David in 2 Samuel 7:11b-17:

These promises were essentially one-sided binding covenants. God initiated both of them and promised to act according to His own character and not based upon Abraham or David's ability to keep the covenants. God said He would create a *people*, enjoying His *provision*, resting under His *protective power*, in a specific *place*. In other words, God promised a kingdom.

Jesus inherited these promises through His family line. In other words, these promises will, according to God, be fulfilled and completed by someone in Jesus' family.

4) Matthew mentioned another era in Jewish history. Fill in the blank below according to verse 17.

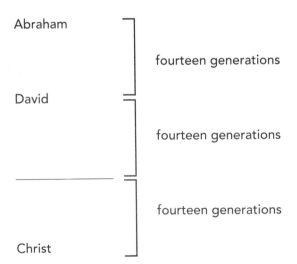

Abraham

fourteen generations

David

fourteen generations

_____

fourteen generations

Christ

In the chart on the previous page, Matthew clearly omitted some names, as his third grouping holds only thirteen names, and 1 Chronicles 3:11-12 lists additional generations. It seems he wanted his readers to focus more on the *arrangement* of the genealogy, specifically the number fourteen. One commentator suggests that the number fourteen is significant because the letters (translated into numbers) of the Hebrew word for "David" add up to fourteen, emphasizing royal kingship. In addition, the number fourteen in the Bible symbolizes completion.[2]

5) By focusing on the number fourteen in relation to Jesus' genealogy, what was Matthew emphasizing to his readers?

6) Matthew's genealogy also includes several women, which is surprising in a patriarchal society. In addition, we might expect to find matriarchs of the faith in Jesus' lineage, such as Eve, Sarah, Rebekah, or Leah. Which women did Matthew include instead, and what does the Bible tell us about them?

PASSAGES	WHAT IS THE WOMAN'S NAME?	WHAT DOES THE BIBLE TELL US ABOUT HER?
Verse 3; Genesis 38		
Verse 5; Joshua 2; Hebrews 11:31		
Verse 5; Ruth 1		
Verse 6; 2 Samuel 11; 2 Samuel 12:11-24		
Verse 16; Matthew 2:11		

7) When the Jews were exiled to Babylon as a consequence for their rejection of God, God promised He would still fulfill the covenants He made with Abraham and David. What do the following prophecies reveal about how this would happen?

- Isaiah 42:1-4:

- Isaiah 53:1-6:

8) Aside from "Son of David" and "Son of Abraham," what are the two additional names attributed to Jesus in Matthew 1:1-17?

- Verse 16:

- Verse 17:

9) The name *Christ* means *Anointed One*. What is the dictionary's definition of *anointed* that best fits the context of this passage?

10) By calling Jesus "the Christ," what conclusion did Matthew reach?

11) Fill in the blue box in the chart according to Matthew's conclusion:

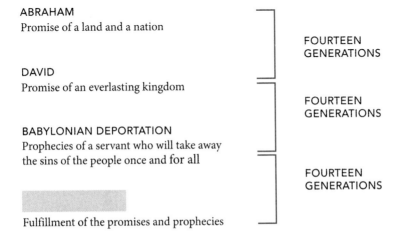

ABRAHAM
Promise of a land and a nation

DAVID
Promise of an everlasting kingdom

BABYLONIAN DEPORTATION
Prophecies of a servant who will take away the sins of the people once and for all

Fulfillment of the promises and prophecies

FOURTEEN GENERATIONS

FOURTEEN GENERATIONS

FOURTEEN GENERATIONS

Matthew, writing to a primarily Jewish audience, started his book by establishing Jesus' familial heritage and, because of His heritage, His inheritance of the promises and prophecies God had made about someone who would be born in His line. Matthew formatted his genealogy in a way that emphasizes how Jesus is in fact the fulfillment of these promises and prophecies. He is the King the Jews had waited for. And He is our King as well.

Apply

Jesus as King means He not only has a title, but He also holds authority. What do you think of when you think of authority? How do you tend to relate to those in authority over you?

Matthew's genealogy takes us through Israel's history of covenants, slavery, sojourn, judges, kings, and exiles. God's people experienced His faithful presence and the fulfillment of His promises, despite their sin, setbacks, and suffering. Looking back at your own personal history, how have you experienced God's faithfulness and promise-keeping despite your sin, setbacks, and suffering?

How has Jesus' service specifically benefited you? Spend time in prayer thanking Him.

Day Two

THE KING'S BIRTH

I enjoy regaling my three teenage boys with the details of their births: my first glimpse of their faces, their first screeches filling the operating rooms, and the first time I held each of them in my arms. I tell them about grandparents, aunts, and uncles gathered around the hospital viewing window and our initial days home with our bundles of joy. In my words, I hope they hear how much they were longed for, prepared for, and how much they've been loved from the moment I knew they were in my womb.

Births are celebrated occasions, noted in family Bibles and remembered each year. Yesterday, we learned about the King's heritage—the grandparents and great-grandparents figuratively standing at the viewing window—and why His heritage is significant. Once Matthew set the stage for Jesus' life being a fulfillment of Old Testament prophecies and promises, he zoomed in on Jesus' nuclear family and the details surrounding His birth— the most significant birth story in history.

READ MATTHEW 1:18–2:23.

1) What are the pertinent facts about Jesus' birth and family?

- Jesus' mother (1:18):

- Jesus' earthly father (1:18):

- Jesus' birthplace (2:1):

- Ruler in power (2:1):

- Jesus' tribe (2:6):

- Jesus' hometown (2:23):

We're told that Mary and Joseph were betrothed. We use this word now to mean "engaged," but in ancient times betrothal was a binding legal agreement, requiring divorce if the agreement was broken. Betrothed couples, however, didn't consummate their marriage or reside together until after their wedding.[3] This explains why Joseph is called Mary's husband and why he could consider divorce rather than merely break an engagement (1:19).

2) What are we told about Joseph's character (1:19,20,24-25; 2:13-14)?

3) What phrase or idea is repeated throughout this section of Scripture (1:22; 2:5,15,17,23)? Based upon yesterday's study, what does this confirm about who Jesus is?

4) Matthew notes explicit details about Jesus' birth that match prophecies made hundreds of years prior about the "Anointed One" God would send. Fill in the chart below.

REFERENCE	PROPHECY	TRUE ABOUT JESUS?
Isaiah 7:14		
Micah 5:2		
Hosea 11:1		

5) What five names are attributed to the newborn in Matthew 1:18–2:23? Note any significant details Scripture attaches to each name.

- 1:21:

- 1:23:

- 2:2:

- 2:4:

- 2:23:

6) The name *Jesus* means "Yahweh saves," and *Immanuel* means "God with us." Who chose Jesus' name? What do these names tell us about Him? What does this tell us about God the Father?

7) What actions are we told Jesus will accomplish in His life?

- 1:21:

- 2:6:

Matthew described where Jesus grew up—Nazareth in the region of Galilee—as a fulfillment of prophecy, but no Old Testament prophecy specifically mentions this detail. Nazareth was a small village, often despised and looked down upon (John 1:46; 7:41).

8) Why do you think Matthew connected Nazareth as fulfilling a prophecy about Jesus? (See Isa. 53:2-3 for help.)

Matthew recorded details from Jesus' childhood that mirror another revered Jewish patriarch's life: Moses. Jesus' family fled to Egypt, just like Moses (Gen. 46:3). Before He turned two, His life was threatened by the nation's ruler, just like Moses (Ex. 1:8-22). Jesus' family fled Egypt according to the Lord's leadership, just as Moses led his (very large) extended family out of Egypt (Ex. 14).

Matthew seemed to foreshadow to his Jewish readers that Jesus would act as a new and better Moses.

9) Look up the following passages and record details from Moses' life.

PASSAGE	MOSES' ROLE OR ACTION
Exodus 3:7-10	
Exodus 3:14-15	Moses was God's spokesperson.
Exodus 4:1-9	Moses was given signs to use to prove he comes on God's authority.
Exodus 12:7-13	
Exodus 12:50-51	
Exodus 14:15-17,26-31	
Exodus 16:4; 17:1-7	Moses gave the message that God has given water and bread from heaven for the people.
Exodus 19:1-6	

10) Why, then, do you think Matthew wanted us to recall Moses when we read about Jesus' birth and childhood?

By attaching specific names and language to the birth of Jesus, Matthew made clear to his readers that this Baby is beyond significant. He is, in fact, the One who will deliver people from sin and death, like Moses saved Israel from Pharaoh's slavery.

Apply

Joseph was told that Jesus "will save his people from their sins" (1:21). Have you been saved from your sins through faith in Him? If not, will you call on Him today? (See p. 222 to understand more of what it means to be saved by Jesus.)

Jesus is our Shepherd, guiding us in the right way to go and providing for our needs. Every single time God directed Joseph through a dream, he immediately obeyed, even when it meant his social embarrassment or uncertainty. Do you put stipulations or conditions on your obedience to God? If so, what are they?

Day Three

THE KING'S INAUGURATION

Most of us live lives of obscurity—learning, serving, and loving in unseen, uncelebrated ways. Jesus wasn't immune to this common human experience. He grew up in obscurity in a tiny village in Galilee, far removed from the center of Jewish religious life in Jerusalem and the religious leaders of the day—the Pharisees and Sadducees.

We can only imagine Jesus' childhood. Perhaps He learned woodworking from His carpenter father and played games with His neighborhood friends. We can imagine how He grew in stature, bypassing His mother in height, and how He took pleasure in His hobbies.

The plan wasn't for Him to remain in obscurity, however. At the appointed time, following the direction of His heavenly Father, Jesus purposefully inched into the spotlight, taking on a public ministry.

Between Matthew 2 and Matthew 3, which we'll study today, about twenty-five years have gone by. Matthew 3 describes the beginning of Jesus' formal ministry. Because He leaves His obscurity behind, willingly seeking the lost for His Father, the world is changed forever.

READ MATTHEW 3.

1) Who was John the Baptist? How does Matthew describe him and what he was doing (vv. 1,4,6)?

2) What else do we know about him from other Gospel writers? Read Luke 1:5-17,39-45 and record what additional details you learn about John the Baptist.

3) Matthew again bridged the Old Testament and the New Testament with his narrative, saying, "For this is he who was spoken of by the prophet Isaiah" (v. 3). The Gospel of Luke also connects prophecies to John the Baptist. Read Luke 1:67-80. Who is speaking? Were these words merely a father's hope for what his son would be? How do you know?

4) According to Matthew 3:3, what was John the Baptist's specific calling from God? What do you think it means to make a path straight? (See Isa. 40:1-5 for help.)

5) What was John the Baptist's message (3:1)?

_____, for the kingdom of heaven is _____.

The "kingdom of heaven" is an interchangeable phrase for "kingdom of God," which you may recall from Day One is a *people* who enjoy God's *provision* and rest under His *protective power* in a specific *place*.[4] As we follow Jesus' life, we will continue to uncover different aspects of this definition.

6) What is the dictionary's definition of *repent*?

7) What do you think John the Baptist meant when he said that the kingdom of heaven is "at hand" (v. 2)?

8) John the Baptist was laying the groundwork for the Anointed One yet to come, preaching that all should prepare themselves to enter into the kingdom of heaven. How did people receive John the Baptist's message? Did he himself receive everyone equally for baptism? Why or why not?

In verses 7-10, John the Baptist specifically addressed the Pharisees and Sadducees. We will see these two groups show up countless times in our study, so it's important that we get to know them.

The Pharisees (meaning "separated ones") studied and strictly observed Jewish law, even down to the minutest of rules they'd developed to help them avoid breaking any commandment of God. They were the strictest sect of Judaism and, therefore, often considered themselves holier than others. They gave such attention to outward minutiae that they sometimes lost sight of weightier matters.[5]

The Sadducees considered themselves true descendants of David's high priest, Zadok. They had wealth, influence, and political power through cooperation with Rome.[6]

9) After reading about these two groups, what do you think John the Baptist meant when he warned them to "bear fruit in keeping with repentance" (Matt. 3:8)? What were these groups *not* doing or getting right in relation to God and others? (For help, compare Matt. 3:9 with Gal. 3:7.)

10) If John was practicing a baptism of repentance, why did Jesus insist on being baptized by him? What does it mean that these are Jesus' first recorded words and His first recorded action in the Book of Matthew (3:15)?

11) What names are attributed to Jesus in Matthew 3?

- 3:3:

- 3:17:

In our reading today, we've observed the King's inauguration—the formal beginning of Jesus' ministry. John the Baptist served as the King's herald. He called on people to prepare themselves for God's Anointed One through repentance, a heart posture worthy of this King. Jesus could not do the work He came to do—to save people from their sins— without people recognizing their need for such a work.

Apply

Give an example of a time when you've repented of sin. What fruit did you see God grow in your life through repentance?

The Pharisees and Sadducees were focused on external rule-keeping but not willing to acknowledge their sin and, therefore, their need for Jesus. Are there areas of your life where you're more focused on rule-keeping than on dependence upon Jesus? How can you better cultivate a reliance on God in those areas of your life?

Day Four

WHO IS THIS KING?

Matthew 1–3 build the argument that Jesus is the Messiah whom God promised to Abraham, David, and the entire Israelite nation. The details of His birth align perfectly with many Old Testament prophecies regarding this Messiah, who would serve God by creating a *people* who enjoy His *provision* and rest under His *protective power* in a specific *place*.

We've already learned some of the ways Matthew described Jesus and connected Him to the Old Testament, but what in His life *confirmed* He was the Messiah sent from God? We're going to skip around in the Book of Matthew today in order to answer this question.

1) Read Matthew 8:1-17 and record your answers to the questions in the chart below.

PASSAGE	WHAT DID JESUS DO?	WHY DID HE DO IT?
8:1-4		
8:5-13		
8:14-17		

What did Jesus exhibit authority over? In what groups of people did He exhibit this authority?

2) Read Matthew 9:1-8 and record your answers to the questions in the chart below.

PASSAGE	WHAT DID JESUS DO?	WHY DID HE DO IT?
9:1-8		

What did Jesus exhibit authority over? In what "group" of people did
He exhibit this authority?

3) Read Matthew 8:23-27; 14:22-33; and 15:32-39. Record your answers
to the questions in the chart below.

PASSAGE	WHAT DID JESUS DO?	WHY DID HE DO IT?
8:23-27		
14:22-33		
15:32-39		

What did Jesus exhibit authority over? In what group of people did He
exhibit this authority?

4) Why do you think Jesus performed miracles of healing, declared sins
forgiven, and displayed authority over the created world?

5) Why is it significant that Jesus performed these miracles among and
for people of various groups and backgrounds?

6) In Luke 4:18-19, Jesus read Isaiah 61:1-3 in the synagogue and attributed it to Himself. Read Isaiah's prophecy about the Anointed One below and underline what we've seen Jesus do and/or groups of people to which He's ministered.

> The Spirit of the Lord GOD is upon me, because the LORD has anointed me to bring good news to the poor; he has sent me to bind up the brokenhearted, to proclaim liberty to the captives, and the opening of the prison to those who are bound; to proclaim the year of the LORD's favor, and the day of vengeance of our God; to comfort all who mourn; to grant to those who mourn in Zion—to give them a beautiful headdress instead of ashes, the oil of gladness instead of mourning, the garment of praise instead of a faint spirit; that they may be called oaks of righteousness, the planting of the LORD, that he may be glorified.
> ISAIAH 61:1-3

Who is this King? Jesus is one with authority over disease and spiritual malaise. And He is a King who exercises that authority for the benefit of those who come under His *protective power*.

Apply

Skim through Isaiah 61:1-3 again. According to your need today, who do you most resonate with: the poor, the brokenhearted, the captive, the bound, or the mourner? How does Jesus specifically respond to the one you most resonate with? Ask Him to meet your need in this way.

The fulfillment of these prophecies shows us that God is a promise-keeping God. What promises are you struggling to believe? Ask God to give you faith where it's lacking.

THE KING'S CROWNING

We expect royal families to act, dress, speak, and live in ways that match their standing. If we ran into the Queen of England eating solo at a local dive restaurant, we'd be sorely disappointed. We'd want to experience her, if we could, in all her pomp and glory. To that end, perhaps to meet the public's expectation and represent their country well, the British royal family must follow specific rules as they interface with their public.

When the Queen stands, no one sits. Royal husbands and wives must not show any public displays of affection. Royals must remain completely neutral on political matters: no voting or making political statements. They can't take selfies or sign autographs, be seen or photographed in casual clothing, and royal women are to wear pantyhose in public. The public is expected to never touch a royal, aside from shaking an extended, gloved hand.[7]

Jesus endured expectations about His kingship as well, and almost no one expected how He'd eventually be crowned King.

So far, we've observed how Matthew named Jesus as the fulfillment of God's promises and prophecies: He was the Anointed One, sent specifically by God to serve, save, and shepherd. By performing miracles and casting out demons, Jesus proved His divine authority over every realm, whether seen or unseen.

However, He also gained followers who believed "the kingdom of heaven is at hand" (Matt. 3:2) meant that the Jewish people would soon cast off oppressive rule and reign in their nation under His authority. Jesus would certainly soon reign, but it would not be in the way they—or anyone else—assumed.

Today, we will move to the bookend that marks the last days of Jesus' life and seek to understand the significance of all He did.

> 1) Why did the Jews believe that if Jesus was truly the Messiah, He would gather them as a nation, overthrow Roman rule, and reign as an earthly king? (See Day One, Question 3 for help.)

2) Who, then, did the Jews believe would be included in the kingdom of God? Who would it exclude?

READ MATTHEW 21:1-11 IN LIGHT OF THE JEWS' EXPECTATIONS OF THE MESSIAH.

3) What did the crowd call Jesus? What significance does this have?

4) What Old Testament prophecy does Matthew reference in this passage that would have reaffirmed the crowd's belief? What does this prophecy call the coming one?

5) All along the way to His entry into Jerusalem, Jesus told His followers they should expect something different than an earthly kingdom. What did He foretell about Himself and what He was really on earth to do?

PASSAGE	WHAT JESUS FORETOLD HE WOULD DO
Matthew 17:9-13	
Matthew 17:22-23	
Matthew 20:17-19	

Jesus' closest friends—Jews themselves—remained confused and bewildered by this talk of suffering, death, and resurrection.

READ MATTHEW 16:21-23 AND ANSWER THE QUESTIONS BELOW.

6) Why do you think Peter responded the way he did?

7) Why do you think Jesus called him Satan?

8) Jesus distinguished between "things of God" and "things of man." In the context of this passage, what are the "things of God" and what are the "things of man"? (See also John 18:36.)

What Jesus foretold about Himself came true. He was tortured, crucified on a cross, and in a grave for three days before He resurrected, overcoming death. (You can read the entire account in Matt. 27:15–28:10.)

9) Read Philippians 2:5-11. What was God the Father's response to Jesus' service?

10) Over whom and what does He now reign?

The servant, through His service, has become King!

The King's crowning ceremony happened in a way the Jews didn't expect. He showed himself to be King, not by taking political power or amassing wealth and influence, but through laying down His life for our sake. This is the King we follow, and we'll see repeatedly in our study of Matthew how Jesus calls us to a similar servanthood.

Apply

Jesus came to serve rather than be served. In what areas of your life are you seeking to be served rather than to serve? What about His example will you emulate today?

Like the Jews and like Peter, we can easily become confused about what Jesus came to do and what He continues to do for His people. What are the "things of man" that often draw your attention away from the "things of God"?

Now that you've studied what Jesus came to do and how He earned His rightful crown from God the Father, consider what you want or expect Jesus to be as King in your life. Does your idea of who He is line up with what He says He came to do?

WRAP UP: *Session One*

The details of Jesus' ancestry and birth point like neon signs to the truth that He is the Messiah God promised Israel. He will go on to save His people from their sins. Through His sinless life, unjust death, and glorious resurrection, He earned the title of King of kings from His Father and currently reigns over the kingdom of God.

The bookends of Jesus' life—His birth and death—are significant and supernatural. The details surrounding them not only prove His divinity, but they also alert us to study carefully what He taught and how He lived while He walked the earth.

What's one main takeaway you learned about the King and the kingdom this week?

How does knowing this truth change the way you relate to God and others?

WATCH THE SESSION TWO VIDEO and take notes below. You can find group discussion questions in the leader guide on page 216.

TO ACCESS THE VIDEO TEACHING SESSIONS, USE THE INSTRUCTIONS IN THE BACK OF YOUR BIBLE STUDY BOOK.

33

ENTERING THE *kingdom*

SESSION TWO

When a couple gets engaged, they are quickly and frequently asked the question: "Have you set a date for the wedding?" With joy and anticipation, we look ahead to the future with them, and while they begin preparations and plans, we wait for the wedding invitation to arrive in the mail. It's then their turn to ask the question: "Will you be there to celebrate with us?"

Invitations to special events always come with a request for a response, because plans are in motion—seats are being saved; food is being catered; and favors are being ordered. The host of the event is making all the preparations; the guest must only RSVP.

In Week One, we learned about the heritage and birth of Jesus Christ and how these fulfilled what had been promised about the coming Messiah. We also learned that Jesus was crowned King by God the Father as a result of His service on the cross. These bookends of His life and what they signify should make us pay very close attention to what Jesus said and did in His life on earth, because He came to us with great intention. He came with an announcement that sounds much like a wedding invitation, and He asks His listeners to respond.

We, as bystanders to the narrative, have the privilege of observing people interact with Jesus and listening in as they recognize how His kingship lays claim to them. As we'll discover, some respond in grateful acceptance to the invitation while others walk away.

The Bible, however, doesn't allow us to remain bystanders. The Holy Spirit reads us as we read God's Word, which is "living and active, sharper than any two-edged sword" (Heb. 4:12). As we study portions of Matthew this week, we'll discover that the kingdom of God lays claim to us as well.

The claim of the kingdom is that there is a King, and we aren't Him. The kingdom claims God-rule and therefore requires we give up all claims to self-rule. The kingdom is a gift, but the King at its center requires that we give up all rights to ourselves and follow Him. We release our hold on ourselves in order to grasp this gift.

Matthew himself had to make the decision of how he'd respond to Jesus. He recorded it in Matthew 9:9: "As Jesus passed on from there, he saw a man called Matthew sitting at the tax booth, and he said to him, 'Follow me.' And he rose and followed him."

Matthew's calling is our calling. Will we, as he and the other disciples did, release all claims to ourselves and take up our places in the kingdom of God? Will we follow Jesus? Will we respond affirmatively to His invitation?

Day One

THE KING'S PROCLAMATION

Announcements are an important part of community life. In church, announcements are given from the pulpit or written in a bulletin so that the entire congregation is aware of the church's mission and can participate in it. In college, announcements for various student groups are chalked on campus or posted on bulletin boards so that students know what's available for them. Even commercials can be considered announcements: a company wants us to know all about their incredible product so that we'll run to the store and purchase it immediately. Announcements, then, can be considered invitations. Will you join the new small group being offered at church? Will you participate in the organization's fundraiser? Will you buy the new product? Announcements imply response.

Jesus came to earth to announce a specific message. Matthew 4:23 says, "And [Jesus] went throughout all Galilee, teaching in their synagogues and proclaiming the gospel of the kingdom and healing every disease and every affliction among the people." Jesus' mission and ministry was to be an embodied announcement from God telling people about the kingdom of God and explaining its message. This announcement wasn't about something private, happening behind palace walls. Jesus' proclamation was an invitation for anyone who heard it to come under God's rule, which is synonymous with His blessing and provision.

Today, as we continue in Matthew, Jesus begins His public proclamation ministry. And as all announcements do, His proclamation demands a response.

READ MATTHEW 4:17.

1) According to Matthew, what is the theme of the proclamation Jesus is giving? Who previously preached this same message? (See Matt. 3:1-2.)

2) You may recall that the kingdom of heaven (or kingdom of God) is a *people* who enjoy God's *provision* and rest under His *protective power* in a specific *place*. Knowing this, what is the invitation in Jesus' message?

3) These are Jesus' first recorded publicly spoken words. Does knowing this affect their importance?

Matthew tells us that Jesus preached this message, implying that He shared this message as He traveled and encountered groups of people. We aren't told about the crowd's response, but we do get a glimpse of Jesus inviting individuals into the kingdom. Let's lean in to hear Jesus' message and each individual's response.

4) Using the verses given below from the Book of Matthew, record what you observe on the chart. (The blue boxes will remain blank.)

	4:18-20	4:21-22	8:19-20	8:21-22	9:9
What is the location?					
Who is called?					
What are we told about them?					
What is Jesus' invitation to the called?					
What does Jesus promise to do for the called?					
What is their response to Jesus' invitation?					

5) What repeated phrase does Jesus use to call these individuals (4:19; 8:22; 9:9)? Using a dictionary, write a definition below of the word *follow* as it relates to Jesus' call.

6) Using the ESV translation, what repeated words did Matthew use to relay how those who became His disciples responded to Jesus?

- 4:20: "_____ they _____ their nets and _____ him."

- 4:22: "_____ they _____ the boat and their father and _____ him."

- 9:9: "And he rose and _____ him."

- By leaving their respective nets, boat, fathers, and tax booth, what were the calculated losses they incurred?

7) Circle the word *immediately* in Question 6. What do you think made these men respond this way when it cost them so much?

- What did they gain?

Not everyone responded to Jesus by immediately leaving all and following Him. In addition, some of the individuals Jesus encountered received a vastly different "call" than the disciples.

READ MATTHEW 9:10-13.

8) Where was Jesus? What was He doing and who was with Him?

9) One of the groups of people with Jesus was a group of tax collectors. Tax collectors were Jews who worked for the Roman government and were known for extorting their own people, which made them despised and considered traitors. What tax collector have we already encountered (9:9)?

10) The Pharisees came to this gathering and labeled the second group the "sinners." Knowing what you know about the Pharisees, what behaviors might have caused a Pharisee to label someone a "sinner"?

11) The Pharisees questioned why anyone would follow a religious leader who ate with sinners. Jesus said, "I came not to call the righteous, but sinners" (v. 13). What did He mean by "the righteous"? Isn't God concerned with our righteousness?

12) To those who became His disciples, Jesus said, "Follow me." To the Pharisees, He said, "Go and learn what this means, 'I desire mercy, and not sacrifice'" (v. 13). How do both of these messages align with Jesus' proclamation, "Repent, for the kingdom of heaven is at hand" (Matt. 4:17)?

13) What types of people has Jesus invited into the kingdom of God?

Jesus invited the people He encountered to experience the kingdom of God, and He said entrance requires that they repent and follow after Him. The same is true for us today. We must turn from whatever personal kingdoms we're cultivating, turn from this earthly kingdom ruled by human tradition and ideas, and turn toward a *greater* kingdom led by our good King. We must come under His rule and reign.

Apply

What do all believers gain when they repent and follow Jesus? What have you gained personally?

How is repentance a gift within the kingdom of God? In what area of your life are you resisting following Jesus? Jesus is inviting and calling you to repent. Respond as the disciples did: leave your sin immediately and follow Jesus.

THE KING'S CONCERN

Jesus came proclaiming God's kingdom. The way to enter, He said, is to repent of all other allegiances and turn and follow Him instead. Men like Simon Peter, Andrew, James, John, and Matthew did just that, but not everyone responded the way they did. We observed in the previous lesson that the Pharisees had reservations about following Jesus. Today we'll take a closer look at one of their interactions with Him, in order to understand their reservations and to see how Jesus responds to these reservations.

In the previous lesson, the Pharisees questioned Jesus' disciples about why they followed a religious leader who ate with tax collectors and sinners, people they considered unclean. Now they've gone straight to the source with their concerns.

READ MATTHEW 15:1-11.

1) What was their primary question to Jesus? What does their question imply about what they thought of Jesus as a religious leader?

The "tradition of the elders" were oral interpretations of the Mosaic Law handed down from and debated by esteemed Jewish rabbis over many generations. These interpretations detailed rules of conduct governing all manner of life.

2) What specific rule were the Pharisees concerned about?

3) Read Colossians 2:8,20-23 and answer the following questions.

• Record synonyms Paul used for the "tradition of the elders."

• What did the "tradition of the elders" promote (v. 23)?

• What could the "tradition of the elders" inherently not do (v. 23)?

4) Returning to Matthew 15, Jesus responded to the Pharisees' question as He often did—with another question. While the Pharisees were concerned with their traditional rules, what did Jesus' question in return show He was concerned with? To what specifically is He referring in verse 4 (see Ex. 20:12)?

5) Fill in the chart below according to Jesus' argument in verses 4-6.

GOD SAID	PHARISEES SAID

In verse 5, Jesus addressed a Jewish tradition of allowing funds set aside for the care of aging parents to instead be declared "corban" (Mark 7:11) or legally "dedicated to God." The funds were then given to the temple treasury, and the Jew would no longer be required to care for their parents.[8]

6) Read verse 5 in the NIV. What specific behavior did Jesus seem to be addressing among the rule-keeping Pharisees?

7) What had the Pharisees elevated to primary authority (v. 6)?

8) Did the Pharisees believe they were following God? What evidence would they have pointed to as support for your answer?

9) If one thinks they are following God because they follow religious rules ("Pharisees say") but his or her heart isn't submitted in obedience to God ("God said"), what does Jesus say this person is (v. 7)?

Jesus used this exchange with the Pharisees as a teaching opportunity for those who genuinely want to learn from Him how to be right with God.

10) In order to be "clean" before God, the Pharisees were depending on hand washing and other external rituals. What did Jesus say is actually the source of our "uncleanness" before God?

READ MATTHEW 15:12-20.

11) What did Jesus call the Pharisees in verse 14? If one were to follow them, where would they be led?

The Pharisees were considered guides because they taught others how to be right with God and how to be considered holy. However, Jesus said they were the blind leading the blind—they themselves didn't know the way. There were two main issues: their hearts were not engaged in their religious practices, and they'd elevated the commandments of men ("Pharisees say") above the commandments of God ("God said"). The Pharisees thought they were following God, but they refused to follow Jesus.

If we don't want to miss the kingdom of God like the Pharisees did, we must learn to fervently follow Jesus, listen to His Words, and obey Him. We must first, however, be cleansed and transformed at the heart-level.

READ GALATIANS 3:10-14.

12) How are we made clean and given access to the kingdom of God?

13) What will not gain us access to the kingdom?

Jesus said there is a way to be right with God, and it's the opposite of what the Pharisees taught. It begins with a clean heart and elevates the commandments of God as authoritative above human tradition.

The Pharisees were offended by Jesus and grew increasingly combative in their interactions with Him. While many will believe and follow Jesus, the Pharisees would remain tethered to their traditions and rituals. Jesus' words about their end are frightening: "Every plant that my heavenly Father has not planted will be rooted up" (v. 13). They were missing the kingdom of God.

Apply

What human ideas, religious traditions, or self-motivated desires do you tend to elevate over the commandments of God?

Jesus indicated that cleanness before God begins in the heart. The Pharisees believed external practices made them clean. What external practices do you often believe will "clean" you? Can any external practices "clean" us?

Day Three

THE KING'S CONFIRMATION

Have you ever experienced doubt regarding the existence or goodness of God? Perhaps you've gone through intense doubt, almost ready to walk away from the faith altogether. Or perhaps you have questions about God or the Bible that remain unanswered and nag at your mind. Doubt is a common experience, even for the strongest of Christians, but doubt is also something that is difficult to admit to other believers.

What about admitting it to God Himself? If you were able to interact with Jesus face-to-face and you mustered the courage to express some of your doubts to Him, how do you think He'd respond? You might think, *Oh, I certainly wouldn't doubt if I could see Jesus face-to-face!* But the Bible records an instance when a man who walked with Jesus and proclaimed Him as the Son of God later began to doubt Him.

So far, as we've seen Jesus call people to enter the kingdom of God, we've read about those who immediately followed Him and those who rejected Him. Today, we'll look at the doubting man who lands somewhere in between, who expressed uncertainty yet sought clarification directly from Jesus. How will Jesus respond to someone with doubts about Him? Let's find out.

READ MATTHEW 11:2-6.

The John referred to in this passage is John the Baptist, the preacher we met earlier in our study. As you may recall, John the Baptist was Jesus' cousin, born with a specific job given to him by God: to "prepare the way of the Lord" (Matt. 3:3b). In other words, he came before Jesus, announcing the King's arrival and calling people to prepare their hearts to follow through the act of repentance. John baptized Jesus in the Jordan River and witnessed the Spirit of God descending on Jesus like a dove.

READ JOHN 1:28-34.

1) What two names did John the Baptist call Jesus in the presence of others?

• Verse 29:

• Verse 34:

2) In John 1, how certain did John the Baptist seem that Jesus was the Messiah Israel had been waiting for? Circle your answer below.

Not very certain   Somewhat certain   Very certain

3) Returning back to Matthew 11:2-6, what did John the Baptist ask Jesus via messenger (v. 3)? Write it below in your own words.

4) How certain did John the Baptist seem now that Jesus is the Messiah? Circle your answer.

Not very certain   Somewhat certain   Very certain

5) Read Matthew 14:3-5 and record why John the Baptist was in prison. Was this a just or unjust imprisonment?

6) Although we're not given the exact reason, based upon what you do know, why do you think John had begun to doubt?

John the Baptist experienced great suffering. He was imprisoned by Herod, the Roman ruler over the region where both Jesus and John the Baptist ministered. The reason for John's imprisonment is found in 14:3-4, where we learn he confronted Herod about his adultery with his brother's wife. For telling the truth and promoting righteousness, John the Baptist faced a death sentence. Perhaps this unjust suffering caused him to despair and doubt.

More likely, John's expectation of what the promised Messiah would do—combined with his current situation—led him to doubt Jesus. John the Baptist, as many Jews did, believed the Messiah would overthrow Roman rule and relieve the Jews from their oppressors. As John sat in prison, he likely wondered when Jesus would overthrow Herod and release him from his chains—and perhaps he was disconcerted as to why it was taking so long.

7) What message did Jesus send to John through John's disciples in Matthew 11:4-5?

"Go and tell John what you _____ and _____" (ESV).

List six things Jesus wanted them to tell John they saw and heard:

1.   4.
2.   5.
3.   6.

8) Jesus' message recalled Isaiah 61:1-2, which we read on Day Four of Week One and is quoted below. If John were to recall this passage, what might stand out to him as sorely missing among Jesus' messianic actions? Underline it below.

> The Spirit of the Lord GOD is upon me, because the LORD has anointed me to bring good news to the poor; he has sent me to bind up the brokenhearted, to proclaim liberty to the captives, and the opening of the prison to those who are bound; to proclaim the year of the LORD's favor, and the day of vengeance of our God; to comfort all who mourn.
> **ISAIAH 61:1-2**

9) Jesus ended His message to John the Baptist with this phrase: "Blessed is the one who is not offended by me" (Matt. 11:6). What do you think He meant by this? With what tone was Jesus communicating?

Jesus' response to John seemed to be a mild rebuke, or at the least a reminder that John must lay aside his expectations of exactly what he hoped the Messiah would be and do. Jesus came for specific reasons, and the miracles He did speak for themselves. Jesus' actions, although amazing, didn't align perfectly with John's expectations, nor the Jews' expectations. They wanted a tangible kingdom that released them from difficult circumstances and brought immediate judgment upon their enemies. They wanted to immediately reign with Jesus over an earthly kingdom.

10) With this in mind, what characterizes a "blessed" person, according to Jesus?

After sending John's disciples off with His message, Jesus turned to the crowds following Him and spoke in glowing terms about John the Baptist.

NOW READ MATTHEW 11:7-11.

11) Why do you think Jesus gave this tribute of John the Baptist after what occurred in verses 1-6?

12) What did Jesus say was the reason people had gone into the wilderness to hear what John the Baptist was saying?

13) Jesus said they were right about John the Baptist. He was not just a prophet. He was the prophet referred to in Malachi 3:1: the messenger preparing the way for the Messiah. Because of this, Jesus used two superlatives to describe John. What are they?

• Verse 9:

• Verse 11:

14) The phrase "born of women" in verse 11 refers to natural human birth. Knowing this, what do you think Jesus meant that no one "born" into the kingdom of heaven is greater than John? How did Jesus seem to define *greatness*?

READ MATTHEW 14:6-13.

15) What happened to John the Baptist in the end?

16) What was Jesus' response?

The Scripture never gives any doubt that John the Baptist was a faithful man. His question to Jesus and the uncertainty behind it didn't upset Jesus, nor did it negate John the Baptist's role and message in preparing the way for the kingdom. Faithful people still may question at times, but they take their questions straight to Jesus, just as John did. Jesus' love and respect for John never wavered.

Like John the Baptist, we too experience frustration and doubt when we lay our expectations on Jesus and demand that He act as we want Him to act. We must know and believe what is *actually* promised to us, as opposed to what *we* think God should do for us. When we do, Jesus says we're blessed: we're given joy by God.

Apply

Read the following passages and write what is promised to us as followers of Jesus:

• Matthew 28:19-20:

• John 16:33:

• Romans 8:35-39:

• 1 Peter 1:3-7:

Doubt isn't the absence of faith. In fact, most genuine believers at times struggle with doubts about God's faithfulness, provision, character, and engagement in the world. When you've faced doubts, what are ways that you "doubted your doubts" and instead cultivated your faith?[9] How were the promises of God a comfort to you?

How has Jesus acted in your life that has been unexpected or difficult to accept? How does John 6:66-68 speak to your doubts or give you words for your doubts?

Day Four

THE KING'S CLAIM

Have you ever experienced the excruciating pain of walking away from someone or something you loved? When my boys were small, we moved thousands of miles away from our extended family. We knew we were obeying the Lord's direction for us, but it was painful to make the willful choice to relinquish close access to grandparents (and babysitting!) and living near our siblings and their children. The move felt costly, sometimes *too* costly.

Twelve years later, we continue to live far from family. The decision to move that many years ago still costs us—there were years in the beginning when I thought to myself, *It's only the gospel keeping me rooted to this place.* However, we've also gained a second home. We've met people we'd never have met otherwise. We've learned how to make the distance work. And we've seen God move in ways we never expected.

Following Jesus is costly. On Day One this week, we met some of the men who left all and immediately followed, and they became for us a picture of how we too are called to respond to Jesus' invitation to enter the kingdom of God. In today's study, we'll meet one of those disciples again—Simon Peter—as well as another man who stands in stark contrast to Peter. We'll watch as King Jesus lays claim to their lives and find that He lays claim to each of us as well. But we'll also find that the King's claim doesn't only require us to "leave all"; following Him also comes with great reward, for Jesus is a King who gives to those who come under His rule.

READ MATTHEW 19:16-22.

1) We're introduced to a nameless man in verse 16. What can we gather about who he was?

• Verse 20:

• Verse 22 and Luke 18:23:

• Luke 18:18:

2) What did this man call Jesus (v. 16; Luke 18:18)?

3) What question did the man ask Jesus?

This entire exchange centers around the man's question: *How do I live eternally with God?* Another version of this question could be, *How do I enter the kingdom of God?*

Jesus responded with a question of His own: "Why do you ask me about what is good? There is only one who is good" (v. 17). Was the man looking for an answer he'd pile on top of all the other answers he received from other teachers? Or would he acknowledge Jesus as God and as the final authority on this question?

4) Summarize the verbal exchange between the man and Jesus in verses 17b-21.

- Jesus (v. 17b):

- Man (v. 18a):

- Jesus (vv. 18b-19):

- Man (v. 20):

- Jesus (v. 21):

5) What synonym for *the kingdom of God* did Jesus use in verse 17? What does this tell us about the kingdom and following Jesus?

6) When Jesus listed the commandments the man must follow, He didn't name all of the Ten Commandments found in Exodus 20. Circle what He *did* mention below.

1. You shall have no other gods before me.
2. You shall not make for yourself a carved image.
3. You shall not take the name of the Lord your God in vain.
4. Remember the Sabbath day and keep it holy.
5. Honor your father and mother.
6. You shall not murder.
7. You shall not commit adultery.
8. You shall not steal.
9. You shall not bear false witness.
10. You shall not covet.

What do the circled commandments focus on: loving God or loving others?

7) Is Jesus' command to the man in verse 21 a literal command we must all follow in order to be "perfect" before God? Explain your answer.

8) What was Jesus' invitation to the man motivated by? (See Mark 10:21 for your answer.)

Jesus was gently addressing the man's need to fulfill the commandments He did not list, namely that the man should have no other gods before the true God. He did not love God with all of his heart. The man's "true love" was revealed in the end, when he walked away sorrowful: he had great possessions he could not let go of in order to gain true riches. The man continued to rely on his wealth for security, joy, and peace—a form of self-sufficiency, and evidence that his heart's allegiance was not to God.

Jesus turned to His disciples in order to help them process what happened in His interaction with the young man.

READ MATTHEW 19:23-26.

9) How can wealth be a hindrance to entering the kingdom of God?

10) Why do you think the disciples—mostly working-class men—were astonished at Jesus' statement that the wealthy will have a hard time entering the kingdom?

11) Verse 26 is a widely repeated phrase. In the context of verses 23-26, what is the "this" that Jesus said is impossible for man but possible with God?

12) Based upon this exchange we've observed, what must we give up in order to enter the kingdom of God?

NOW READ MATTHEW 19:27-30.

13) What did Peter leave in order to follow Jesus? (See Matt. 4:18-20 as a reminder.)

14) Fill in the chart below with what Jesus says those who follow Him gain by doing so:

VERSE(S)	GAINED IN THIS AGE	WILL GAIN IN THE AGE TO COME
19:28		
19:29 (see also the added phrase in Mark 10:30)		
19:30		

15) In what period of time do we experience the costs of following Jesus? Circle your answer(s).

In this age   In the age to come

16) In what period of time do we experience the rewards of following Jesus? Circle your answer(s).

In this age   In the age to come

17) Who are the hundredfold people added to us now at this time? (See Eph. 2:19-20 for help.)

18) How are these people a gift or reward for us? Look at the following verses to answer the question:

• 1 Corinthians 12:26-27:

• Hebrews 10:24-25:

The kingdom of God is an invitation to life. To enter, we leave all other gods, including the god of self. Self-reliance, self-justification, self-sufficiency—all of these are like trying to squeeze a camel through a needle's eye. Entry is only gained through perfectly obeying the commandments of God, and we're not able to do that. Our King, as we'll soon discover in detail, does what is required for us to enter the kingdom!

Apply

The man held onto his wealth as his security and sufficiency. What are you trying to hold onto that is keeping you from loving God with all your heart? Is this giving you true life, peace, or joy? How will you respond to this awareness today?

The church is a reward and gift to us because others help us bear the costs of following Jesus and provide a tangible reminder that there is an eternal reward waiting for us.

- Do you view the church as your reward? Why or why not? How could you better give and receive this gift?

- What have you learned from others around you regarding the costs of following Jesus? What has watching others leave all and follow Him done for your own faith?

Day Five

THE KING'S INVITATION

This week, we've focused on Jesus' interactions with various people and how, in conversation with them, He's invited them to enter the kingdom of God. Some have gone after Him immediately, some have rejected Him, and one has questioned Him with genuine concern. Today, we will discover the specifics of the invitation Jesus gives to those He's interacting with. What is He inviting them to experience? And how is that invitation ours as well?

On Day Three of this week, we observed how John the Baptist inquired of Jesus in Matthew 11:3: "Are you the one who is to come, or shall we look for another?" Jesus responded with a gentle rebuke, followed by a glowing tribute to John. Today, we pick back up in chapter 11, just after this tribute concluded.

READ MATTHEW 11:16-24 FOR CONTEXT.

Jesus turned toward the crowd around Him and seemed to say, "Don't miss it! Don't miss the invitation I'm offering you!" There were some who were stubborn and combative (vv. 16-19), and there were some who were pridefully unrepentant, even though they had seen Jesus' miracles (vv. 20-24). As we've already learned, Jesus is looking for a specific response: repentance—to turn from the earthly kingdom and self-sufficiency and follow Jesus. Repentance opens wide the kingdom of God to us.

Jesus says to all who will listen that our souls will be required of us. We must not act as if the judgment (vv. 22,24) isn't a reality sometime in the future. We must be wise now in this time and consider our souls. We must consider whether our allegiance is to an earthly kingdom we can see or the as-yet-fully-seen kingdom of God. We must carefully consider Jesus' invitation.

After addressing the unrepentant, He detailed this invitation.

READ MATTHEW 11:25-30.

1) Verse 25 says, "Jesus declared," but then He seemed to speak to God the Father as if in prayer. How would you characterize what Jesus was doing here?

2) What are "these things" that Jesus said God has hidden from the wise and understanding?

3) Who are the "wise and understanding" to whom Jesus was referring? (See 1 Cor. 1:26-29 for help.)

4) Jesus said the truths about the kingdom of God have been revealed to little children. Explain what He meant.

5) Read the following passages and record what you see regarding children and their understanding of the kingdom of God.

Passage	What characteristic(s) of children did Jesus favorably point out?	What or who did Jesus connect with children?	What did Jesus want His hearers to emulate in the children?
Matthew 18:1-4			
Matthew 19:13-15			
Matthew 21:14-16			

6) In Matthew 11:16-17, Jesus used an example of children in a negative light as He talked about the religious leaders and others who have rejected Him as the way into the kingdom of God. What characterizes these "children"?

Jesus contrasted those who are wise according to the world (and thus proudly self-sufficient) with those who are needy and who, recognizing their need, depend upon someone else for their provision. Jesus often used children as an illustration of how we're to identify ourselves in relation to God the Father and the kingdom He is building.

7) Returning to Matthew 11:25-30, read verse 26 in the NIV. Why do you think Jesus said this aloud? What was He conveying?

8) What did Jesus reveal about God the Father?

• Verse 25:

• Verse 26:

• Verse 27:

9) What has Jesus revealed about Himself?

• Verse 27:

• Verse 29:

• Verse 30:

10) Fill in the chart below based upon what Jesus said in verses 28 and 29.

WHAT JESUS SAID WE'RE TO DO	WHAT JESUS SAID HE DOES

11) Read verse 28 in the NIV. Using a dictionary, write a definition for the words below that best fit their usage in the verse.

• *Weary:*

• *Burdened:*

12) Fill in the blank below for what Jesus said we find in Him (v. 29b):

"You will find _____ for your _____" (ESV).

How might a person become weary or burdened in her soul?

Jesus said that a person experiences soul rest when she takes on His yoke. A yoke is a device connecting a beast of burden, such as an ox, to a plow. Oxen labor to pull heavy weights under such yokes. Jesus says the yoke He places on people is easy and the burden He asks them to carry under this yoke is light. This would have come as good news to a people led by the religious leaders of their day. Jesus says in Matthew 23:4 that by adding their own rules to the Law, the religious leaders "tie up heavy burdens, hard to bear, and lay them on people's shoulders." He adds, "woe to you, scribes and Pharisees, hypocrites! For you shut the kingdom of heaven in people's faces" (v. 13).

The self-sufficient carry a burden and, likewise, place it on others. This burden is heavy and wearisome, because the security of eternal salvation and standing with God rests upon his or her labor.

13) What is Jesus' yoke? Record your insights from each passage below.

• John 6:28-29:

• Colossians 2:13-15:

• 2 Corinthians 5:21:

Jesus, in contrast to the religious leaders of the day, opens the kingdom of heaven to people by inviting them to take on His yoke. Security of eternal life and right standing with God rests upon His labor rather than our own, thus freeing the soul and giving peace and joy. What is His becomes ours.

> 14) The kingdom of God is a *people* who enjoy God's *provision* and rest under His *protective power* in a specific *place*. How does Jesus' invitation in Matthew 11:25-30 demonstrate the kingdom of God?

Come. Take. Learn.

The King's invitation is to *come* under His provision for your soul. He doesn't turn us away in our need. In His invitation to follow Him, Jesus invites us to consume Him that we might find sustenance for our souls.

Jesus is also a King who invites us to *take* from Him—in other words, He gives of Himself. He takes our weary burdens of trying to prove ourselves or make ourselves good enough for God and gives us rest from these labors in return. This doesn't lead to spiritual apathy or laziness; a true understanding of this grace leads to worship and obedience.

Finally, Jesus is a King who invites us to *learn* from Him. He describes Himself as gentle and lowly of heart, so from Him we learn humility, compassion, and mercy. The invitation to learn from Jesus is an invitation to a transformed and joy-filled life.

Apply

> We enter the kingdom of God as children, but we don't remain children. Jesus' imperatives to come, take, and learn help us grow spiritually. Of the three, what do you need to integrate or cultivate more in your life? How will you implement this into your life this week?

> In what areas of your life are you stubbornly self-sufficient? What would it look like for you to turn to Jesus in dependence as a child in that specific area?

WRAP UP: *Session Two*

The invitation of the kingdom is to come into it by faith in Jesus. He is the gate, the door, the way—and there is no other. He is King. And the good news—the news Jesus Himself proclaimed—is that He's done everything on our behalf that's needed for entrance to the kingdom. We were dead in our sins, making us unacceptable in our unrighteousness to enter in, but He in His righteousness took the punishment for our sins so we could enter in. Not only did He remove our sins from us, but He also welcomed us into a kingdom by sharing His riches with us. We enjoy the kingdom's peace, joy, love, and hope. Everything that is the King's is ours, including the favor and approval of God Himself.

What's one main takeaway you learned about the King and the kingdom this week?

How does knowing this truth change the way you relate to God and others?

WATCH THE SESSION THREE VIDEO and take notes below. You can find group discussion questions in the leader guide on page 216.

TO ACCESS THE VIDEO TEACHING SESSIONS, USE THE
INSTRUCTIONS IN THE BACK OF YOUR BIBLE STUDY BOOK.

61

THE

culture

OF THE
KINGDOM

SESSION THREE

Have you ever traveled to a country vastly different from your own and experienced feelings of culture shock? Several years ago, my husband and I were privileged to travel halfway across the globe in order to teach and encourage gospel workers. As soon as I exited the plane, the sights, sounds, smells, and tastes both intrigued and overwhelmed my senses. I felt a heightened awareness of my out-of-place presence everywhere we went, and as I attempted to learn basic phrases and culturally appropriate mannerisms in order to connect with people, I felt like a toddler learning to walk. Home felt far away.

When we returned home, however, I suddenly could see my own culture through the lens of the outsider. Although I quickly fell back into life at home, I had a newfound appreciation for cultures different from my own.

The kingdom of God is a collection of people with a specific culture. Although we can't see it and don't experience it fully yet, if we're in Christ, we're already living as citizens of this kingdom. The culture of the kingdom of God is difficult to grasp because we can't see God. The kingdom of God is so upside down and inside out compared to the earthly kingdom we live in.

The one way we can grasp the culture of the kingdom is to look at Jesus Himself and how He related with God the Father and the people around Him, for He is an embodied announcement from God about the kingdom. What did He say? What did He do? What did He love, and what did He condemn? As we learn more and more about how to walk as Jesus' disciples while we live in this upside-down world, God is, by His Spirit, acclimating us to His kingdom's culture and transforming us into kingdom citizens.

Now that we've learned how to enter the kingdom of God, over the course of the next two weeks of study, we'll explore the *culture* of this kingdom. The challenge will be wrapping our hearts and minds around a culture that is so foreign to the earthly kingdom we live in.

We will study Matthew 5 this week, and the words will likely be familiar to you. However, as we study Jesus' famous words through the lens of the kingdom, my prayer is that we will see and understand them in a new and profound way. Most importantly, we must consider if our lives actually reflect the kingdom of God as Jesus describes it. Are its priorities our priorities? Do we believe and show with our actions that true life is found within the culture of the kingdom? These are the questions we'll answer this week. Let's get started.

Day One

THE KINGDOM'S BLESSING

If I were to ask you to name the conditions under which life would be best for you, what would you say? If you're like me, my mind immediately goes to certain circumstances I'd like to see become a reality in my life. These are circumstances that seemingly promise safety, security, comfort, sure outcomes, and happiness—things like financial security, deep friendships, a loving church, and a pain-free life for my children.

But how would Jesus our King answer that question? What is the best life according to Him? He gives us some ideas about how life works best in our passage today. You may recall that as Jesus began His public ministry, He called several men to follow Him: Simon Peter, Andrew, James, and John. They immediately left their fishing nets and became His disciples.

READ MATTHEW 4:23-25.

NOW THAT WE HAVE THIS CONTEXT, READ MATTHEW 5:1-12.

1) Matthew set the scene for us. Record the details he gave below.

• Where did this scene take place?

• Why did it take place here?

• Who was on the scene?

Matthew mentioned that Jesus was seated. Rabbis in those days taught from a seated position, which signified their authority. Matthew wants us, as his readers, to equate what Jesus was about to say with authoritative truth and wisdom.

2) In verse 3, Jesus began to give His most famous sermon, what we often call the Sermon on the Mount. This sermon begins with a section known as the Beatitudes. *Beatitude* means "supreme blessedness or happiness." Why do you think Jesus gave this sermon to His disciples and not also to the crowds that flocked to Him?

Jesus repeated two words or phrases throughout this section: "blessed" and "kingdom of heaven." We've already defined the kingdom of heaven (or kingdom of God) as a *people* who enjoy God's *provision* and rest under His *protective power* in a specific *place*. We now must define this oft-used word *blessed*. The Greek word used here (*makarios*) is defined as "a believer in a fortunate position from receiving God's extended provisions and favor."[10] Being a blessed person implies a state of secure well-being and joy that cannot be touched, shaken, or stolen away based upon circumstances.

Perhaps Jesus preached this message of blessing to the disciples alone, because they already had chosen to come under His authority. He wanted them to know what specific blessings were theirs under His rule and provision. We, too, must hear this message: to submit to the rule and reign of Jesus as King is to come under His provision and favor. It is to know supreme joy. In His teaching, Jesus told the disciples what blessings are available to those who follow Him. Let's turn now and dissect His words.

3) Fill in the chart below according to Jesus' sermon to the disciples.

VERSE(S)	Who receives blessing under the rule of Jesus?	What specific blessing do they receive from Him within His kingdom?
5:3		
5:4		
5:5		
5:6		
5:7		
5:8		
5:9		
5:10		
5:11-12		

4) How would you define being *poor in spirit*, or put a different way, spiritually impoverished?

5) What specifically do we mourn that God promises to comfort?

• 1 Corinthians 15:24-26:

• 2 Corinthians 1:3-5:

• 1 John 1:9:

6) Look up *meek* in a dictionary and write the definition below. What does it mean to be meek?

7) What does it mean to hunger and thirst for righteousness? Look up the references below to help with your answer.

• Psalm 42:1-2:

• Jeremiah 15:16:

8) Considering those who come under the rule and reign of Jesus are spiritually impoverished (v. 3), can we then make ourselves hungry and thirsty for righteousness, merciful, pure, or peaceable? Is this a choice we make and something we discipline ourselves to do? Or are these things evidence of work done in us? Explain your answer.

9) Are the blessings you wrote down in the chart on Question 3 blessings that we receive now or sometime in the future? On the left side of the chart, mark the following:

☐ Put a check next to the blessings that we experience now.

☐ Put a heart next to the blessings that we will experience in the future.

☐ Put a star next to the blessings we can experience now and will also experience in the future.

What insights do you gather from this exercise?

10) Let's consider the earthly kingdom in contrast to the kingdom of God. What kinds of people does the earthly kingdom in which we live esteem? Revisiting the chart on Question 3, write the antonyms of the characteristics Jesus says make a person blessed on the right side of the chart.

11) Now read Luke 6:24-26 and write Jesus' repeated phrase in the blank: _____.

What repeated phrase from Matthew 5:1-12 does this contrast with?

Jesus described internal qualities in today's passage. Purity of heart and a hunger for righteousness certainly show through external works, but Jesus was noting an essential truth about the kingdom of God: It is cultivated by God Himself in the heart of each person who comes under the rule and reign of Jesus.

The second truth Jesus communicated about the kingdom of God is that Jesus' rule is one of provision and blessing. He gives a joy we ourselves can't manufacture, and because it happens internally and separate from earthly circumstances, it remains through such earthly experiences as persecution and suffering.

Finally, Jesus communicated that the kingdom of God will one day be seen. It will move from an internal reality in the hearts of believers to a tangible reality we can see and fully experience. This is the ultimate blessing for those who bow to Jesus as King.

Apply

Which of the blessings Jesus named do you struggle to see as a blessing?

How does knowing the kingdom of God is partially hidden now but will be fully realized one day help you embrace each of these as blessings?

As human beings, we tend to struggle with the idea of coming under someone else's rule. How has submitting to God's rule in your life been a source of joy for you?

Day Two

THE KINGDOM'S CULTIVATION

When my oldest son turned nine, we took him and several of his friends to Chuck E. Cheese. As a part of the party package we purchased, Will received an inflatable birthday crown and a chance to win tickets in the highly anticipated Ticket Blaster. Wearing his inflatable birthday crown and goggles, Will stepped into the tube, and the attendant closed the door while dramatically adding special tickets—some worth fifty points, some one hundred, and one that was worth a whopping one thousand points. His friends pushed their hands and noses against the glass, the attendant turned on the blaster, and suddenly Will appeared to be fighting a tornado. He flailed his arms, trying to capture as many tickets as he could, laughing hysterically. Then, in unison, we noticed the one thousand-point ticket had lodged itself into Will's inflatable crown. *He had it!* Now all he had to do was keep it, but he was oblivious to his success.

We started screaming at the top of our lungs, "It's in the hat! It's in the hat!" Unable to hear us above the noise of the machine, he repeatedly bent over, grabbing at tickets, and we repeatedly moaned in agony, fearful the ticket would plummet to the ground. Finally, after what seemed like years, the machine stopped, and Will stepped out of the tube with the treasured ticket still clinging to his crown.

It was in the hat, his all along.

In our passage today, Jesus told His disciples that there were certain things about them that were "in the hat"—things that were true about them because they had been pronounced as "blessed." Being a blessed person opens up to us an internal well-being and joy that is eternally secure—far more secure than a ticket in an inflatable birthday crown. As Jesus continued His sermon, He told His disciples that if we know this internal well-being is ours and that it's secure, it leads to specific external practices. We act upon what has been gifted to us.

LET'S READ MATTHEW 5:13-16.

In verses 1-12, Jesus described the realities of the kingdom of God, most of which we will experience in the age to come. In verses 13-16, He focused on the present day—this earthly kingdom. He described His plan for cultivating and spreading the unseen kingdom of God throughout the earthly kingdom. We see this in His choice of words: "the earth" (v. 13) and "the world" (v. 14). His plan for kingdom cultivation involves His disciples participating in kingdom work. In other words, He's commissioning His disciples.

1) What do you think of when you hear the oft-used term "kingdom work"?

2) Jesus used two "names" for the disciples. What are they?

• "You are _____" (v. 13).

• "You are _____" (v. 14).

Circle the phrase below that best conveys the meaning of Jesus' words.

• You are becoming salt and light. • You will one day be salt and light.

• Work to become salt and light. • You already are salt and light.

3) What specifically has made the disciples "the salt of the earth" (v. 13) and "the light of the world" (v. 14)? (Hint: Consider the definition of *blessed* we learned on Day One of this week.)

4) Salt in biblical times was a basic commodity but also very valuable. Fill in the chart below to discover what salt was used for or symbolic of.

PASSAGE	SALT USED FOR OR SYMBOLIC OF
Leviticus 2:13	
2 Chronicles 13:5	

The covenant of salt was connected both to the priests' offerings in the tabernacle and to David, the one promised an everlasting kingdom. Salt represented permanency and preservation. For the offerings, salt represented holiness and purity. In addition, newborn babies were bathed in water mixed with salt, because it was thought to have medicinal benefits, and farmers used it in small doses as fertilizer.

5) What do we primarily use salt for today?

6) Now that we have a deeper understanding of both the practical and symbolic uses of salt, why do you think Jesus called His followers "the salt of the earth"?

Jesus warned the disciples against losing their saltiness. Salt, or sodium chloride, cannot actually lose its taste. However, in the first century, the way salt was derived made it very impure. The sodium chloride could easily leach out, leaving a substance that lacked salty taste. This substance was considered completely useless and would be thrown out.[11]

In Matthew 5:1-12, Jesus detailed the blessings for those who come under His rule and reign. Our verses today turn toward the follower's responsibility.

7) As the salt of the earth, what is our responsibility? In other words, how might our "saltiness" become so diluted that we become ineffective in the kingdom? (See Mark 9:50 for help.)

Now let's turn our attention to the second name: "light of the world."

8) READ JOHN 8:12.

- Who else is named the light of the world?

- What is this light called in verse 12?

- For Jesus to call His followers this name as well, what was He communicating to them?

Because there was no electricity in biblical times, light was as valuable as salt. Sunlight was essential to the workday, and candlelight enabled people to see and move about with clarity after sundown.

9) Biblical writers often used light and darkness in symbolic ways. Fill in the chart below with what symbolism they convey.

PASSAGE	WHAT DOES LIGHT SYMBOLIZE?	WHAT DOES DARKNESS SYMBOLIZE?	ARE WE GIVEN A COMMAND? IF SO, WHAT?
John 3:19-21			
Romans 13:11-13			
1 John 1:5-7			

10) With a deeper understanding of the biblical symbolism of light and darkness, why do you think Jesus called His followers the light of the world?

11) In Matthew 5:14, Jesus said a city on a hill, by nature, cannot be hidden. As the light of the world, then, what does verse 16 tell us about our responsibility?

Later, in Matthew 6, we'll read about how Jesus taught His disciples that they should *not* pray, fast, or do good deeds as the Pharisees do—that they may be seen by others (6:5,7,16). In Matthew 5:16, however, Jesus said they should "let their light shine before others."

12) Why do you think Jesus condemned some public acts but commended others?

While the Pharisees focused on external practices, Jesus says that internal realities—a heart submitted to Him—lead to a transformed life that will worship God through good deeds. These good works are a response of love, because we enjoy the benefits and blessings of His loving rule. We are, by nature, now salt and light, and as we live according to our new nature, we become instruments the King uses to cultivate His kingdom.

Apply

How does knowing you *already are* the salt of the earth and the light of the world cause you to view your life and your place in God's kingdom?

Are there areas of your life in which you're loving darkness more than the light? How is this affecting your relationship with God your Father? How is this affecting you and those around you? Confess your sins to God and a trusted friend.

In relation to salt and light, the biblical writers give two specific commands regarding our speech. Read Philippians 2:14-15 and Colossians 4:6. Then think about how you are using your words in your closest relationships. Where do you need to add "salt"? How does knowing that God is patient, forgiving, and gracious toward you inform your speech patterns and offer you help in adding this salt?

Day Three

THE KINGDOM'S LAW

Most modern kings and queens don't write or enforce laws. The Emperor of Japan, for example, plays a largely ceremonial role and holds no political power. As a member of a family dynasty that's continued since the AD 500s, he is primarily a symbol and representative of the state, attending cultural events and welcoming representatives from other countries.

The kingdom of God is entirely different. King Jesus is not a symbol or a ceremonial leader. Not only does He give the governing laws, He is the living law of the kingdom. He embodies what the law requires.

So far this week, as we study the culture of the kingdom of God, we've learned how the King blesses those in His kingdom and how He cultivates His kingdom through His work in and through His followers. Today we will listen in as the King declares the *law* of His kingdom.

Recall the scene: Jesus and His disciples had left the crowds and retreated to a mountaintop. Jesus sat, as all revered rabbis do, to convey His wisdom and authority. The disciples gathered around Him, and Jesus taught them specifically about how the kingdom of God works.

READ MATTHEW 5:17-20.

1) Let's define the terms Jesus used in verse 17.

• What does the word *abolish* mean? Using a dictionary, write the definition below:

• What are "the Law and the Prophets"? (Hint: The Torah, or the first five books of the Old Testament, is often called the Law.)

2) Using your own words, write what Jesus was saying in verse 17:

3) The dictionary lists several definitions for the word *fulfill*. Place a check by any of the definitions below that indicate what Jesus came to do in regard to the Law and Prophets.

☐ To carry out or bring to realization
☐ To obey or follow commands
☐ To satisfy requirements
☐ To finish or complete
☐ To develop the full potential of

4) How does one enter the kingdom of heaven, according to Jesus (v. 20)?

Remember, the Pharisees and the scribes studied and strictly observed Jewish law, even down to the minutest of rules they'd developed that would help them avoid breaking any commandment of God. They took pride in their external religious practices, but Jesus said over and over in Matthew that they had impure hearts. Jesus was telling His disciples that they must be righteous at the heart level in order to enter the kingdom of heaven. This is a hefty requirement.

5) How do we ensure God will call us "great" in the kingdom of heaven?

6) Can we fulfill what Jesus is asking? Write Galatians 3:10 below as an answer to the question.

Unless we accomplish *all* of the Law perfectly, we're cursed. We can't enter the kingdom, much less be great in the kingdom. We don't know the disciples' response as they listened to Jesus, but perhaps they heard these requirements and shook with fear, knowing the state of their hearts and lives. I certainly would hear this concept for the very first time with fear and dejection as I examine my life.

We must understand, then, not what Jesus is saying about His followers, but rather what He is saying about *Himself*.

7) Look carefully at verse 18. What did Jesus say is to be accomplished?

8) The words *fulfill* and *accomplish* are similar. Who does the work of fulfilling and accomplishing the Law in full?

Israel's kings were given specific commands regarding the law:

> And when [the king] sits on the throne of his kingdom, he shall write for
> himself in a book a copy of this law, approved by the Levitical priests.
> And it shall be with him, and he shall read in it all the days of his life,
> that he may learn to fear the LORD his God by keeping all the words
> of this law and these statutes, and doing them, that his heart may not
> be lifted up above his brothers, and that he may not turn aside from
> the commandment, either to the right hand or to the left, so that
> he may continue long in his kingdom, he and his children, in Israel.
> **DEUTERONOMY 17:18-20**

Kings were meant to instruct their citizens in the law, internalize the law themselves, embody the law, and write just legislation that helped people thrive and obey the law themselves. Kings, in other words, were to be living embodiments of the law: both instructing and modeling what it meant to follow the law. The king's subjects, then, were meant to imitate their king.[12] As the king went, the nation went as well.

Many Old Testament passages convey this idea, with both negative and positive examples. King Solomon disobeyed the Lord by marrying foreign women who didn't worship God. Because of this, his heart became divided, and the kingdom was subsequently torn in two. A divided heart led to a divided kingdom. When other kings tore down places of idol worship, their subjects returned to worship the Lord. As the kings went, the nations went as well.

Marrying these two ideas—that kings were meant to give and embody the law and that where the king goes so also goes the kingdom—gives us new insight into what Jesus is saying about Himself in Matthew 5:17-20.

JESUS GIVES AND EMBODIES THE LAW.

In future days of our study, Jesus will connect the old (Old Testament law) with the new (kingdom law). He will say, "You have heard it said," while referencing an external religious practice. Then He will say, "But I say to you," in reference to internalization of the law leading to obedience. He is not establishing a new law, but He is rather detailing the *heart* of the law as God originally intended it. As King, He teaches the law.

He also embodies the law, demonstrating by example how to be a citizen of God's kingdom.

9) Complete the chart below to show how Jesus exemplified wisdom.

PASSAGE	WHAT DID JESUS TEACH IS A KINGDOM LAW?	PASSAGE	HOW DID JESUS DEMONSTRATE THIS TRUTH HIMSELF?
Matthew 5:4		Matthew 23;37	
Matthew 5:5		Matthew 11:29; 21:5	
Matthew 5:7		Matthew 9:13	
Matthew 5:10		Matthew 27:23	

Finally, Jesus is the Living Law, meeting the law's demands and therefore fulfilling it. This is what Jesus referred to when He said before His death, "It is finished" (John 19:30b). He accomplished His mission. This won His Father glory and His Father, in turn, crowned Him as King. But the King did something in winning the kingdom: He shared it with us!

WHERE THE KING GOES, SO GOES THE KINGDOM.

Because Jesus fulfills the Law perfectly, this has significant implications for His followers. He's removed us from the kingdom of darkness and delivered us into His kingdom. He's redeemed us, forgiven our sins, and made us the very righteousness of God. The curse of sin is removed. (For more, see Col. 1:13-14; 2 Cor. 5:21; and Gal. 3:13-14.)

Jesus is a King who gives! What's His becomes ours as well: His blessing, His righteousness, His inheritance. What we could not do—obey the Law perfectly—He did for us.

Jesus also gives us the ability to internalize and obey God's Word through His indwelling Spirit. As the King's subjects, He empowers us to imitate our King out of love for our King.

Apply

Looking at the chart on Question 9, what did Jesus demonstrate that is most difficult for you to imitate?

As you struggle with this, do you tend to look at your own ability to "fulfill" or "accomplish" obedience or to the truth that Christ fulfilled perfect obedience and then offered that standing before God to you?

How does considering Christ's work rather than your own ability to change spur loving, worshipful obedience?

Day Four

THE KINGDOM'S
LAW CLARIFIED

As a child, one of my favorite book characters was Amelia Bedelia. Amelia worked as a housekeeper for the Rogers family and was forever getting into fixes because she took their instructions literally. She's told to make a cheesecake, so she decorates a block of cheese with icing. She's told to remove the spots on Mrs. Rogers's dress, so she cuts out the polka dots from the pattern of the dress with scissors. When she's told to plant new bulbs in the garden, she sticks light bulbs in the ground. Somehow, despite her wacky literalness, she wins the Rogers over at the end of each book and is never fired from her job.

Amelia Bedelia and the Pharisees have a miss-the-point literalness in common. The Pharisees were far more focused on the strict meaning of words and actions given in the Mosaic Law and doing just enough to fulfill those requirements, rather than seeking to know and love God with all their heart, soul, mind, and strength. They missed the point of the law entirely—both why it was given and the heart of the One who gave it.

Today's passage begins to describe the "why" behind the "what" of the law, giving us a peek into the heart of God the Father. Jesus will say, "You have heard it said," referencing an Old Testament command, and then He will say, "But I say to you," and describe obedience to this command as something that happens in the heart. As we discovered yesterday, He was not establishing a new law, but He was rather detailing the heart of the law as God originally intended it. The "why" behind the "what" is the heart of God.

LET'S FIRST RECALL THE CONTEXT OF TODAY'S PASSAGE.

1) On Day Three, we studied Matthew 5:17-20, with a focus on the fulfillment of the Law and Prophets. Who fully accomplished the law?

Just as yesterday's passage was primarily about Jesus, today's passage is as well. This is important to note, because we often read this section of Jesus' sermon as what to do and not to do—a checklist of impossible demands. This passage, however, expands on exactly what Jesus perfectly fulfills, and also what we as His followers will love and do by His power because we love Him.

We will see two repeated phrases in the study today and tomorrow: "You have heard it said," followed by, "But I say to you." When Jesus said, "You have heard it said," He meant, "You have understood," or "You have literally understood."[13] In other words, the Pharisees misunderstood and misapplied the law. They developed rules and rituals based upon the law, but they missed the heart of the law. In saying, "But I say to you," Jesus offered them a true reading of the law.

2) Read Matthew 5:21-26 and fill in the chart below according to what you read.

What had they "heard it said"?	
Which of the Ten Commandments was Jesus referring to (see Ex. 20)?	
How did Jesus expand His listeners' understanding of this commandment? What sin did He say breaks this commandment? ("But I say …")	
What examples did Jesus use to illustrate how a person who truly understands and obeys this commandment might act?	
What two types of relationships are pictured here?	

3) Jesus addressed anger and shouting an insult that displays contempt for another. Write the dictionary's definition below for these two terms:

Anger:

Contempt:

4) Who enacted judgment in the following verses, man or God?

• Verse 21:

• Verse 22:

5) Why is unrighteous anger so destructive to the kingdom of God? (See Jas. 1:20 and 4:1-2.)

6) The kingdom of God, Jesus said, condemns hate-filled anger that destroys relationships. What does this tell us about the heart of God?

Then Jesus moved on to another "You have heard that it was said."

7) Read Matthew 5:27-30. Fill in the chart below based upon what you read.

What had they "heard that it was said"?	
Which of the Ten Commandments was Jesus referring to (Ex. 20)?	
How did Jesus expand His listeners' understanding of this commandment? What sin did Jesus say breaks this commandment? ("But I say ...")	
What examples did Jesus use to illustrate how a person who truly understands and obeys this commandment might act?	

8) If one were to literally take out an eye or cut off a hand, this wouldn't eliminate the sin of adultery and lust. What, then, was Jesus saying to us about obeying this commandment?

In the ancient world, a married man could have sexual "adventures" as long as they did not involve a married woman (which would mean violating the rights of her husband). A woman, however, was expected to have no such relations. The command Jesus cited makes no distinction; people of both sexes were to remain faithful in marriage. Specifically, He spoke of the man as the adulterer.[14]

9) By addressing adultery and lust in this way, what did Jesus communicate about the heart of God the Father? What does He communicate about what the kingdom of God condemns?

10) Now read Matthew 5:31-32 and fill in the chart below based upon what you read.

What had they heard it said?	
What law was Jesus referring to? (See Deut. 24:1-4 and Jer. 3:1.)	
How did Jesus expand His listeners' understanding of this law? What sin did He say breaks this commandment? ("But I say ...")	

Divorce and remarriage are complex topics. In this passage, Jesus didn't touch on the entire scope of God's directives on divorce. He did, however, express God's heart about marriage and divorce. Even religious people during biblical times had a fairly cavalier attitude toward divorce.

11) What did Jesus communicate about the heart of God the Father regarding men, women, and marriage? What does this communicate about what the kingdom of God condemns?

12) Why is divorce destructive to the kingdom of God? (See Eph. 5:31-32.)

Most of us have in some way been affected by a person's failure to keep these commandments or our own failure to keep them. Most of us have also been affected by someone else's failure to reflect the heart of God behind these commandments. Perhaps you've been demeaned or devalued as a woman; perhaps your spouse has been unfaithful; perhaps you've been blamed for the lust of another or used sexually as the object of lust; or perhaps you've been the target of anger or contempt. God is grieved that His heart wasn't reflected in your relationships with others, and we can be sure that His kingdom won't include any of this dehumanization and pain.

Apply

How have you or those you love been affected by anger, lust, or unlawful divorce? Why were these so destructive?

How does God's heart reflected in these clarified commandments bring you comfort and hope?

If you were the perpetrator of anger, lust, or unlawful divorce (and all of us have been guilty of one or more at one point or another), how does knowing Jesus fulfilled the law perfectly on your behalf bring you comfort and hope? How does it compel you toward repentance and obedience?

Day Five

JESUS, THE LIVING LAW

Yesterday, we listened in as Jesus began to clarify the Law for His disciples. He said that obedience to the Law must occur not just in behavior but in our hearts and minds, which we also discovered is an impossible task for us. Thankfully, Jesus is the Living Law, fulfilling it perfectly on our behalf and giving us His Spirit to lead and empower us to obey it. The kingdom law shows us not only what Jesus fulfills but also the heart of God the Father, both what He values and what He condemns.

In our study today, Jesus continues clarifying the Law. He uses the same language we observed yesterday: "you have heard that it was said," in reference to Old Testament Law, and "But I say to you" as the introduction to His clarification of God's intention of that law.

1) Read Matthew 5:33-37 and fill in the chart below based upon what you read.

What had they "heard ... said"?	
What law was Jesus referring to? (See Lev. 19:11-12 and Num. 30:1-2.) So which of the Ten Commandments was Jesus referring to? (See Ex. 20.)	
How did Jesus expand His listeners' understanding of this command? ("But I say ...")	
What examples did Jesus use to illustrate how a person who truly understands and obeys this command might act?	

Jesus taught His disciples that the Old Testament Law is clear: one should not lie and should certainly not lie using God's name as an oath. But Jesus takes it one step further. He says that, for a kingdom citizen, oaths should not be necessary at all. A disciple's *character* should speak for herself. Disciples should both speak and live according to truth.

2) Why are lying and duplicity so destructive to the kingdom of God? (See Rom. 2:23-24.)

3) Now read Matthew 5:38-42 and fill in the chart below based upon what you read.

What had they "heard ... said"?	
What law was Jesus referring to? (See Deut. 19:16-21.) So which one of the Ten Commandments was Jesus referring to? (See Ex. 20.)	
How did Jesus expand His listeners' understanding of this commandment? ("But I say ...")	
What examples did Jesus use to illustrate how a person who truly understands and obeys this commandment might act?	

4) In Jesus' examples, who was He addressing? The lawbreaker who had borne false witness or the one who had been falsely accused?

5) What did Jesus call the lawbreaker in verse 39?

6) Did Jesus contradict God's original Law? Explain your thinking.

According to God's Law, His people have a legal right to justice when wrongs have been done against them. Jesus does not discount this right. In the context of His sermon, however, He addresses the heart of the Law, which is perfect justice. As humans, in our striving for justice, our hearts can easily turn vengeful. We desire God-like power in order to judge and punish the wrongs others have done against us. Jesus calls His disciples to refrain from vengefulness and retaliation—a heart matter. Instead of retaliation, we're to return evil with kindness and goodness (Rom. 12:21).

7) Why is sinful vengefulness so destructive to the kingdom of God? (See Rom. 12:19; 1 Cor. 6:1-8; Gal. 5:13-15.)

8) Read Matthew 5:43-48 and fill in the chart below according to what you read.

What had they "heard ... said"?	
What law was Jesus referring to? (See Lev. 19:18.) So which one of the Ten Commandments was Jesus referring to? (See Ex. 20.)	
Which part of the law they had been taught was not actually in the original Ten Commandments?	
How did Jesus expand His listeners' understanding of this commandment? ("But I say ...")	
What examples did Jesus use to illustrate how a person who truly understands and obeys this commandment might act?	

9) What are we to "put off" and "put on"?

10) What did Jesus communicate about God's character?

11) Why do you think loving our enemies is a core value within the kingdom of God?

As we conclude our study of Matthew 5:17-48, it's important to note that Jesus bookends this section with two important truths:

> Do not think that I have come to abolish the Law or the
> Prophets; I have not come to abolish them but to fulfill them.
> **MATTHEW 5:17**

> You therefore must be perfect [*in all these commandments*],
> as your heavenly Father is perfect.
> **MATTHEW 5:48**, *italics mine for clarification*

Jesus says our hearts must match the heart of the Father, loving what He loves and obeying what He says. We know ourselves and therefore know that this is impossible for us. But what is impossible for us is not impossible for God.

Jesus, the Living Law, fulfilled these perfectly. He didn't just speak truth, He lived it in a way that embodied His name "the truth" (John 14:6). When He stood trial, facing death, He didn't defend Himself, nor did He remove Himself from the cross as true justice called for. He died an unjust death so that we might be counted just and right before God. This injustice is to our great benefit. And, finally, He loved His enemies and persecutors, dying even for them. He was perfect, and as the King goes, so we go in His kingdom. We're given, by His grace, right standing before God—as if we were perfect in all the commandments.

Apply

As kingdom citizens, we're to emulate our King's obedience to the law.

How did Christ endure unjust suffering? (See 1 Pet. 2:20-24, especially v. 23.)

In what ways are you holding on to past offenses done against you?[15] How are you cultivating vengeance in your heart or acting in retaliation? What would it look like for you to entrust yourself to the just Judge?

Are you living deceptively in any area of your life? What do you need to confess and repent of in order to live in obedience to your King?

WRAP UP: *Session Three*

Jesus has invited us to a life of blessing under His rule. This blessing is to receive His righteousness, provision, and power in order that we can obey and emulate His life. The kingdom He is cultivating is happening in the hearts of those who submit to His rule, and though it stands starkly opposed to our earthly kingdom, He has shown us how the kingdom law reflects the very heart of God the Father. He is a just Judge. He loved us when we were still His enemies. He is merciful, and He sees and responds to the spiritually impoverished.

As a result of His heart implanted within us, we have a part to play in spreading the culture of this kingdom. We're His servants, salt of the earth and light within the world, displaying His goodness for all to see.

What's one main takeaway you learned about the King and the kingdom this week?

How does knowing this truth change the way you relate to God and others?

WATCH THE SESSION FOUR VIDEO and take notes below. You can find group discussion questions in the leader guide on page 216.

TO ACCESS THE VIDEO TEACHING SESSIONS, USE THE INSTRUCTIONS IN THE BACK OF YOUR BIBLE STUDY BOOK.

LIVING THE
kingdom
LIFE

SESSION FOUR

What wonderful knowledge it is to know, as we discovered last week, that the King gives that which the kingdom of God requires! No longer do we stand condemned but rather we stand approved and accepted before God because of what Jesus did for us. Our account has been filled with the riches of Christ's mercy and grace. Nothing can separate us from the love and approval of our Father in heaven.

But what about the daily things of life? Don't you sometimes wonder what the kingdom of God means for your every day? I do. When I hear a sermon about the beauty of the gospel, thankfulness wells up in my heart. But then I leave church and head into the minutiae and stress of a typical week of work, responsibilities, concerns, uncertainties, and difficulties. Is the kingdom of God mostly concerned about my secure future in heaven but not relevant to those things?

Sometimes we might wonder if God is engaged in daily life with a sense of being too needy. Perhaps we keep coming to God with the same old thing, falling into the same sin, or wrestling with the same doubt. We worry we may be getting on God's nerves. Does He really care about the things that we care about?

However, sometimes we ask if God is engaged in the daily things of life out of a sense of frustration, anger, or entitlement. We wonder where God is and why nothing is going our way. We wonder if God is truly good or if He set the planet in motion and then left us to fend for ourselves.

The daily things of life are where our worry and distraction exist, where fear and anxiety live, so we need to know how the kingdom of God impacts these moments and feelings. We need to know how to live the everyday kingdom life, because living the kingdom life is for our ever-increasing joy.

In our study this week, we'll discover what it means to live according to the culture of the kingdom in our everyday disciplines and practices. And Jesus will repeatedly tell us that God the Father is far more engaged in our lives than we could possibly imagine.

His provision for His people is profound.

Day One

THE KINGDOM WAY OF GIVING

Have you ever been in on a happy secret? I think fondly of the happy secrets in my life, like the time I was told by a friend that she'd recently started dating a wonderful man, or when I served as a job reference for a friend and the employer let me in on the news they'd already decided to hire her. My favorite happy secrets, however, are when my pastor-husband is asked by donors who want to remain anonymous to tell specific people in our church that their needs have been taken care of. What a delight we both get when he describes to me the recipient's reaction! There is something about the secrecy of it all that adds to our joy and encourages us to consider how we can anonymously bless others as well.

In today's passage, we continue eavesdropping as Jesus speaks with His disciples. He pivots from discussing heart matters to discussing specific examples of a disciple's obedience that will flow out of a heart devoted to God. The theme of His instruction is not just happy secrecy but also *holy* secrecy, and, specifically today, the joy of secret giving.

1) Read Matthew 6:1 and write it below in your own words.

This verse is Jesus' theme for the first few days of this week's study. He will give several examples, each meant to support this theme, so it's imperative that we dissect these words.

2) Read Matthew 6:1 in the NIV. What two words did Jesus use to caution His listeners?

3) What do you think the phrase "practicing your righteousness" means?

4) What allegiance or motivation was Jesus warning us away from as kingdom citizens?

5) What did Jesus not want His disciples to miss out on?

Jesus cautions against any behavior that does not come from a heart of love and worship toward God. We aren't to go through religious motions just because it's the "right" thing to do or live morally in order to maintain our reputation before others. We must "be careful" to engage our hearts in relationship to God. True obedience flows out of a heart devoted to God and is led and empowered by the Holy Spirit.

To help His listeners consider the implications of this teaching, Jesus gives an example of what He's talking about.

READ MATTHEW 6:2-4.

6) Fill in the chart below with as many details as you see in verses 2-4.

WHAT THE HYPOCRITES DO (OR "WHAT NOT TO DO")	WHAT KINGDOM CITIZENS DO (OR "WHAT TO DO")
Their Motivation:	Their Motivation:
Their Reward:	Their Reward:

7) What does Jesus assume each person, whether a hypocrite or a kingdom citizen, will be doing?

8) Most commentators think the phrase "sound a trumpet" is figurative. What do you think Jesus means by this phrase? What might "sounding a trumpet" look like in our modern world?

9) The word *hypocrite* was used for actors who played a part and whose words were spoken for effect and not in order to convey the truth.[16] What is the hypocrite's actual concern in the act of giving money to the poor? What is the kingdom citizen's concern?

We read Matthew 6:1 as the theme statement of this section of Jesus' message to His disciples. The other bookend statement, which we'll return to in the following days, is an elaboration on this theme. Let's look at it together.

READ MATTHEW 6:19-21.

10) How do these verses serve as a "bookend" for Matthew 6:1?

11) We tend to read this passage as a caution against hoarding money or collecting physical possessions (which is accurate), but what are some intangible things the world treasures in addition to physical possessions? (Hint: What do the hypocrites value and work for in Matt. 6:1-4?)

12) What is the end of these earthly treasures?

13) What are "treasures in heaven"? In other words, what does God treasure? Read the following verses and record what you discover.

PASSAGE	WHAT GOD TREASURES
1 Timothy 4:8	
1 Timothy 6:6-8	
Hebrews 11:6	

14) What does Matthew 6:20 tell us about these heavenly treasures?

To conclude, Jesus addressed what concern might be growing in His disciples' minds as they listened to His sermon. They knew their hearts, and therefore knew that they did treasure things on earth. As human beings, wrapped in flesh, their allegiance was divided. How could they set their heart's allegiance fully on the King and His kingdom? Jesus said, "For where your treasure is, there your heart will be also" (Matt. 6:21).

Jesus told the disciples that when they treasured rightly, their hearts would follow closely behind. Practicing our obedience in secret—for God's eyes alone—trains us to treasure rightly and, through this, God grows our wholeheartedness. We will increasingly learn to value what He values, and we'll rejoice that we will one day be rewarded by our Father. This is a reward that lasts, unlike the fleeting approval of men or the easily lost reward of money.

Jesus tells us that we're to be careful in how we live as kingdom citizens. We're not to live as the world lives, striving after what they value and crave. However, we must note that sometimes the outward behavior for hypocrites and kingdom citizens may look the same: both may give to the poor. It is the heart motivation behind this act that matters, because it is what God sees. Our hearts of faith must align with our works of faith.

Apply

Is your Christian life more characterized by doing the "right things" (external behaviors) or rather by seeking to love Christ for who He is (internal affections)?

Does Jesus intend the truth that "your Father who sees in secret" to strike fear, as in *get it together*, or to bring comfort? Explain.

Not all earthly treasures are bad. In fact, God gives us gifts in this life that He means for us to enjoy, such as friendship, creative cultivation, and creation. Our enjoyment of these gifts glorifies Him when they remain in their proper place. What are signs that otherwise good gifts in this life have taken the place of God in our heart's allegiance?

Day Two
THE KINGDOM WAY OF PRAYING AND FASTING

We usually think of secrecy in negative terms. We discovered yesterday, however, that there is a holy secrecy that God treasures, a holy intimacy between ourselves and the Lord that leads to our obedience. This theme of holy secrecy will remain at the forefront as Jesus continues His sermon with a well-known section on prayer. Though you may have read or repeated what we call the Lord's Prayer many times, it's important that we see Jesus' model prayer through the lens of the kingdom of God.

As we begin, let's recall together Jesus' theme statement in Matthew 6:1. Write it below from the NIV.

In Day One, the example Jesus gave to illustrate His theme statement was about giving money to the poor. Today, He will give two more examples: one about prayer and the other about fasting.

1) Read Matthew 6:5-6 and fill in the chart below regarding prayer.

WHAT THE HYPOCRITES DO (OR "WHAT NOT TO DO")	WHAT KINGDOM CITIZENS DO (OR "WHAT TO DO")
Their Motivation:	Their Motivation:
Their Reward:	Their Reward:

2) As He did in Matthew 6:1-4, Jesus referred to "the hypocrites." According to Matthew 23:13, who are the hypocrites?

Using your own words, write a definition for *hypocrite* below.

3) Did Jesus condemn all public prayer? Does all prayer have to occur in a private room? Explain your answer.

4) Record the phrase Jesus repeated from His first example of holy secrecy in Matthew 6:1-4:

"And your _____ will reward you" (ESV).

5) Jesus said, "Pray to your Father who is in secret" (v. 6b). What do you think it means that God the Father is in secret?

The Jews had prescribed times to offer certain prayers, and Jesus condemned those who would "happen" to find themselves in a public place at those times, to be seen and admired by others. Prayer for those hypocrites was not an interaction between an individual and God but rather a performance before an audience of their peers.

Jesus didn't just condemn the hypocrites' prayer. He also cautioned His disciples about praying like a second group of people, the Gentiles. Gentiles were non-Jews, and some Gentiles believed in pagan gods.

READ MATTHEW 6:7-8.

6) What did the Gentiles do in prayer that they thought would earn them a hearing from their god or gods? Record what Jesus told His disciples not to do in each of these translations of Matthew 6:7.

• ESV:

• NIV:

• NASB:

7) What truth about God the Father did Jesus tell us in verse 8?

8) If God knows what we need before we ask Him, why do we pray?

After condemning prayer for show and prayer full of meaningless, repetitive babble, Jesus gives His disciples an example of commendable prayer. This prayer is personal, intimate, and succinct. This prayer is a prayer of submission to the rule of God in our hearts. Let's study it together.

READ MATTHEW 6:9-15.

9) What does this prayer teach us about God the Father and what He does for those submitted to His rule?

10) What does this prayer teach us about ourselves and what we need within the kingdom of God?

11) This prayer is a prayer for heart alignment with the kingdom of God. What did Jesus express are the values of the kingdom?

Now we come to the third example Jesus gave in Matthew 6 of how we're to practice holy secrecy.

READ MATTHEW 6:16-18.

12) Fill in the chart below regarding fasting.

WHAT HYPOCRITES DO (OR "WHAT NOT TO DO")	WHAT KINGDOM CITIZENS DO (OR "WHAT TO DO")
Their Motivation:	Their Motivation:
Their Reward:	Their Reward:

In Jesus' day, various fasts were observed, but the Old Testament Law only required one fast, which occurred on the Day of Atonement (see Lev. 16:29-34). The Day of Atonement was an annual observance, during which the priest would enter the Holy of Holies and make a sacrificial atonement for the sins of all of Israel. On this day, God required the nation of Israel to observe Sabbath rest and to fast from eating food. The Day of Atonement was a serious, somber day as the nation reflected on their sins and their need for forgiveness and restoration before God.

Jesus didn't condemn fasting; in fact, He assumed His disciples would fast. He said when they did, they should anoint their heads and wash their faces, meaning they should erase any sign of what they'd done in secret before the Lord. However, unlike the instruction on how to pray, He didn't give any further details on how a disciple should fast, perhaps because fasting is a physical representation of a longing and need for God, and Jesus was present with them. (See Matt. 9:14-15.)

The New Testament writers later deemphasize preoccupation with certain foods or abstaining from certain foods. Why is that?

READ ROMANS 14:17 AND RECORD IT BELOW.

Paul reiterated Jesus' point: the kingdom of God is concerned with matters of the heart. As Jesus' disciples, we enjoy an intimate relationship with our Father. From that relationship will come true obedience.

13) What phrase does Jesus repeat for emphasis in Matthew 6:18?

"And your _____ will reward you."

Repentance, prayer, fasting, and obedience—all of these are seen, valued, and rewarded by our good Father.

Apply

When it comes to prayer, do you tend to think you have to "earn" a hearing from God by the manner or length you pray? How do Jesus' words speak to your prayer life?

What one phrase from the Lord's Prayer sticks out to you as one you need to pray for heart realignment?

Are you preoccupied with food? Or do you connect food with your righteousness before God? How does Romans 14:17 realign your priorities?

THE KINGDOM WAY
OF TRUSTING GOD

When difficulties, uncertainties, or frustrations in your life arise, what is your typical go-to response? Does anger flair? Irritation? Do you run to food or drink as a numbing medication? Are you prone to despair, paralyzed by it all?

My *modus operandi* is control. In my mind, I make a list of ways I'll attack the problem. If I can stay ahead of emotion by simply staying in motion, I believe I can keep further problems at bay and perhaps even solve the issue at hand.

No matter our response to difficulty, what lies beneath is usually fear. And any response to fear that seeks refuge in other people, physical things, or self is antithetical to the reality that we have a benevolent King and belong to His kingdom.

As Jesus has called us to cultivate holy secrecy that leads to joyful obedience, He has reiterated for His listeners that the kingdom of God is concerned with the hearts of people. The kingdom of God is growing and building as people like us submit our hearts to King Jesus, so turning in trust to Him with our fears and concerns is an important practice for every disciple. Wherever He rules and reigns is where the kingdom of God exists and thrives. And, as we'll see today, when our hearts are bowed in allegiance to King Jesus, we come under the watchful care and perfect provision of our heavenly Father.

READ MATTHEW 6:22-24.

In Jewish literature, the eye is often synonymous with the heart.[17] In Ephesians 1:18, Paul used similar language, when he prayed for his friends to have the eyes of their hearts enlightened. In order to understand what Jesus was saying, then, read verses 22-23a again, replacing *eye* with *heart*:

> The [heart] is the lamp of the body. So, if your [heart]
> is healthy, your whole body will be full of light, but if your
> [heart] is bad, your whole body will be full of darkness.
> **MATTHEW 6:22-23a**

A healthy heart or eye leads to spiritual enlightenment or clear spiritual vision. An unhealthy heart or eye means utter spiritual blindness.

1) In order to make a point, Jesus made several stark contrasts in verses 22-24. Note His contrasts below by filling in the blue blanks in the chart.

Health	versus	Unhealthy
Light	versus	
	versus	Hate
Devoted	versus	
Serve:	versus	Serve:

Jesus' point was that we can't have divided loyalties within the kingdom of God. The word He used—*cannot*—is a strong word meaning "sheer impossibility."[18] He wasn't saying that a true disciple won't struggle with his or her loyalties or face temptations toward lesser allegiances. He was saying that only one loyalty is true and right for the kingdom citizen, and only one leads to health and light for the heart. He was also saying that we can't have it both ways; we can't cultivate a love for worldly allegiances at the same time we cultivate a love for God. Choosing a worldly allegiance is choosing to reject and despise God.

To illustrate His point, Jesus once again referred to money. If we cultivate a love of money, He said, we become a slave of money. This is a false king that promises what it can't actually fulfill: security, peace, happiness, and a sure future. When we love money and seek after its false promises, it instead becomes a terrible taskmaster.

In contrast, Jesus invites us to look with the eyes of our heart at what serving God means. When we choose to give our undivided loyalty to God, we choose a Ruler who *does* fulfill what He promises. The security, peace, and joy we crave are actually found in Him, because He is a God who gives of Himself to us. That's where Jesus turns our attention now—to gaze at our heavenly Father and learn how He relates to us.

READ MATTHEW 6:25-34.

2) What commands did Jesus give His disciples in these verses?

3) What command did Jesus repeatedly emphasize?

4) Look up Matthew 6:25 in the Amplified Bible version using an online Bible tool. What additional words does this version give for anxiety?

5) What five things were the disciples specifically told not to be anxious about? Next to each one, note if they are necessities, optional "wants," or potentially both.

- Verse 25:

- Verse 25:

- Verse 25:

- Verse 27:

- Verse 34:

6) What do you think Jesus meant when He asked, "Is not life more than food, and the body more than clothing" (v. 25)? Based upon the details of Jesus' sermon so far in Matthew 5–6, what should we concern ourselves with or prioritize above food and clothing?

7) In order to illustrate to His disciples why they should not be anxious about these things, Jesus used two "much more" examples. Record your insights about these examples below.

8) Jesus said His disciples were "of little faith" (v. 30b). Do you think this is a rebuke or simply a declarative statement about the frailty of being human? Explain your answer.

Jesus said there are some things we don't need to think about. It's not that we just *shouldn't* think about these things, but that we *don't need* to think about them because *someone else is thinking about them for us.* That Someone is God. He's on it. When the responsibilities were meted out, He willingly signed up for the job of provision. He's attentive toward our physical needs for food, water, and clothing. He's attentive toward our emotional needs for value and significance. He's attentive toward our limits of time and space, our todays and tomorrows.

Anxiety, then, is misplaced attentiveness. An attentiveness to needs we ourselves are thoroughly unable to fill leaves us, consequentially, with shaky confidence. Anxiety is not productive or powerful to change anything. When we give our minds over to it, however, it feels as if just by thinking about a circumstance, we can change it, or that if we worry about the future enough, we can affect or prevent misfortune. Anxiety makes God appear small, uncaring, and untrustworthy—a disengaged or even an absent Father.[19]

9) Jesus taught that, as kingdom citizens, we must be attentive to what cultivates a confidence in God. According to Matthew 6:25-34, what is God doing and attentive toward?

10) Verse 33 is well-trod. Now that you've read it in context, what do you think Jesus meant when He commanded us to "seek first the kingdom of God"? (For help, consider our working definition for the kingdom of God and see also Matt. 6:10.)

11) What will be given to us, according to verse 33? Do you think Jesus meant food and clothing will be given to us or something more?

12) How does Matthew 6:11 connect with Matthew 6:34? What does Matthew 6:11 give us as a framework for responding to worry?

Our anxiety will always lead us to tomorrow, next week, and next year, but it never takes us far enough into the future. "The future" to us is what happens within our lifetime. The future Jesus spoke of was the fulfillment of the kingdom. When He says, "Seek first the kingdom" (Matt. 6:33), He's reminding us there is an end to this life and all the clothes and food and money we pine after. Jesus said we should think ahead to the kingdom, precisely so we might keep our perspective in check about what really matters and what's really worth giving our time and mental energy toward. In other words, we should be attentive to our true security: a place in God's family forever, an inheritance that cannot be taken away, and a God who will never fail us and whom we will one day see face-to-face.

As we do this, what will grow? We will experience the peaceful simplicity of not needing to hold onto much of anything in this life, except what actually matters.

Apply

What concern or worry do you need to bring under the rule and reign of Christ ("seek first the kingdom") instead of your own rule and authority (anxiety)?

Go outside and consider creation. What does creation—your heart beating, the trees rooted in the ground, the baby in a womb, birds flying, waves crashing onto the shore—teach you about God? What do those truths mean for your life and concerns today?

Scripture holds additional "much more" passages that convey how much God's provision surpasses our need. Read Romans 5:15-17 and notice the "much more" phrases. What does King Jesus provide for you? How does this speak to your worries about the future?

Day Four

THE KINGDOM WAY OF
RELATING TO OTHERS

So far, much of Jesus' sermon has expounded on what He calls the first and greatest commandment, found in Matthew 22:37: "You shall love the Lord your God with all your heart and with all your soul and with all your mind." Jesus told His disciples that their heart's allegiance must be to God alone.

He now will begin expounding on the second greatest commandment: "Love your neighbor as yourself" (Matt. 22:39). Jesus called the second greatest commandment "like" the first, meaning a wholehearted trust of God the Father will be reflected in how we love others. What we love and value most (God) shows itself in our lives and in the way we relate with others (neighbor).

And as Jesus said in Matthew 22:40, "On these two commandments depend all the Law and the Prophets." This language recalls Matthew 5:17: "Do not think that I have come to abolish the Law or the Prophets; I have not come to abolish them but to fulfill them."

Jesus continued to explain the way of the kingdom of God. That "way" involves how we love our neighbors.

LET'S READ MATTHEW 7:1-6.

1) Jesus explained kingdom law to His disciples. According to verse 1, how were they not to wield this law in relation to others?

2) What happens to the one who wields the kingdom law as a weapon against others?

Jesus' use of the word *hypocrite* in verse 5 should sound familiar. He was once again teaching His disciples by pointing at the Pharisees as an example of what to avoid doing.

3) To gain a better understanding of what sort of judgment Jesus referred to in this passage, look up the following verses and record your insights as to how the Pharisees were relating to others.

• Matthew 23:1-3,4,13:

• Romans 2:1-5:

4) Based upon your study of these passages, whose rightful place of judgment were the Pharisees taking?

5) What were they specifically pronouncing judgments about regarding their fellow man?

6) Returning to Matthew 7:1-6, how were the disciples to rightly wield kingdom law (v. 5)?

• First:

• Then:

• What part of the Lord's Prayer in Matthew 6:9-13 corresponds with this truth?

Did you notice that there is a place for judgment in the kingdom of God? The Pharisees had placed themselves in the place of God, pronouncing whether or not others had done what was required to enter God's kingdom. They valued their knowledge and ritualistic observance of the Law above obedience to God and loving their neighbor. They were wielding the Law as a weapon.

The judgment to which Jesus positively referred is different. Remember, He was explaining to His disciples what it means to love their neighbor as themselves. Therefore, we know the sort of judgment He commends is loving judgment.

7) What relationship is depicted in verses 4-5?

8) Let's dig deeper into what the Bible commends as loving judgment among our spiritual family. Read the following passages and record your insights.

• 1 Corinthians 5:9-12:

• James 5:19-20:

9) What do all those receiving judgment in these passages have in common?

Loving judgment is not putting ourselves in God's place as ultimate judge; it is gently and humbly seeking to restore someone we love to God. Aside from placing ourselves in the ultimate judgment seat, the Bible condemns another type of judgment among our spiritual family.

10) According to Romans 14:1-4, what kinds of concerns are we not to judge our brothers and sisters in as a display of love?

LET'S CONTINUE IN JESUS' SERMON TO HIS DISCIPLES. READ MATTHEW 7:7-11.

11) How does this passage naturally flow from what Jesus said about judging others? (Hint: It may help to consider what often motivates our judgment of others.)

12) What did Jesus tell us about who God the Father is and what He does? List as many details as you can find in this passage.

13) If we understand and believe the truths Jesus conveyed to us about God the Father, how will that naturally affect the way we relate to others?

READ MATTHEW 7:12.

Matthew 7:12 is Jesus' summary statement for the section of Scripture we've studied today. It is also synonymous with the second greatest commandment: "Love your neighbor as yourself" (Mark 12:31).

14) Write Galatians 5:14 below. Circle the "one word" that is our command in how we relate to others.

It's been said that we should first focus on loving ourselves before we can truly love others, but Jesus assumed that we already love ourselves, and we do. We naturally seek good for ourselves, feed ourselves, keep ourselves warm, and protect ourselves. We don't have to be told to do these things. We do, however, need supernatural help loving others in this same way. Thankfully, God has given us His Spirit, who enables us when we call upon Him to love others in imitation of the way He's loved us (Gal. 5:22; 1 John 4:19).

Apply

Our earthly kingdom bristles at any inkling of judgment and often uses Matthew 7:1 as the basis for rejecting a standard of right or wrong. Does the idea of God as Judge give you peace or cause you fear? Explain.

When it comes to judgment, do you tend to consider and evaluate others more than you allow God to search and test your own heart? How do Jesus' words in Matthew 7:1-6 challenge you today?

What do you want or need from God the Father that you've been hesitant to bring to Him? Ask Him for it today.

Day Five

THE KINGDOM WAY IS CAREFULLY CHOSEN

Near our home, there are countless trails weaving through woods, near streams and a winding river, leading explorers by huge rocks, perfect for boys to climb on. On one walk through the woods, my husband and sons went looking for a certain familiar stream crossing and, instead, got lost. On this unfamiliar trail, they stumbled upon a set of old grave markers and two large stone chimneys. By decoding the dates and names on the grave markers, they determined the family had lived in these woods during the time of the American Civil War and had lost several of their children in infancy. Kyle and the boys couldn't wait to return home, tell me about their find, and bring me deep into the woods to see it all for myself. So they made careful note of the route they'd taken, using natural markers to help them return.

When the boys took me out, they chose each step carefully until we found the grave markers. Sometimes we'd stand at a crossroads and they'd discuss what they remembered the natural markings to be, deliberating the right way to go. Life is characterized by many winding paths to choose from. Comparable to how my boys deliberately considered their steps, we must consciously and carefully choose our way, because only one path leads to life.

For two weeks now, we've studied Jesus' sermon that He gave to His disciples on the top of a mountain, often called the Sermon on the Mount. Today we will study Jesus' concluding words in His sermon.

START BY READING MATTHEW 7:28-29.

1) What detail did Matthew add that lets us know the scene of the sermon has changed since Jesus began speaking in 5:1?

2) What did the crowds recognize in Jesus (v. 29)?

As we read Jesus' concluding statements, we can almost sense Him shifting His focus to the larger crowd, extending the invitation to enter the kingdom of God to those who were curiously listening at the periphery.

3) Read Matthew 7:13-27. Jesus made four contrasts, each one illustrating two categories of people. Record your insights below.

PASSAGE	WHAT TWO THINGS DID JESUS CONTRAST?	ACCORDING TO THIS CONTRAST, WHAT DID JESUS WANT HIS LISTENERS TO DO?	WHAT DID JESUS CAUTION HIS LISTENERS ABOUT?
7:13-14			
7:15-20			
7:21-23			
7:24-27			

Jesus lays out the choice each person has in life: there is one way that leads to spiritual life and health, fruitfulness, being known and loved by God the Father, and endurance. And then there's another that leads to spiritual destruction and disease, uselessness, not being known by the Father, and an inability to withstand suffering. He once again invited His hearers to follow Him, to come under His rule and blessing, and to enter into the approval of the Father through Him.

We should read Jesus' words and ask God to test our faith, for we certainly don't want to be the one who says, "Lord, Lord," assuming our entrance into the kingdom of heaven only to find that we'd missed Him entirely. Let's look at the commands Jesus gave as a litmus test for our own lives.

4) Write Jesus' commands to them below. (Hint: See vv. 13 and 15.)

5) Where can we find the narrow gate? (See John 10:7-10.) Jesus said the gate is narrow and the way to life is hard. How is entering the kingdom through Jesus hard for us?

6) What characterizes a false prophet, making them difficult to recognize?

7) What fruit do false teachers exhibit that give them away? Look up the following verses and list as many bad fruit as you see.

VERSE(S)	BAD FRUIT OF FALSE TEACHERS
Titus 1:16	
2 Peter 2:1-3,14, 18-19	
1 John 4:1-6	

8) Why should we be careful whose teaching we follow? (See vv. 21-23.)

9) What fruit do kingdom citizens exhibit that give them away? Look up the following verses and list as many good fruits as you see.

VERSE(S)	GOOD FRUIT OF KINGDOM CITIZENS
Matthew 7:24	
Galatians 5:22-23	

Not all roads lead to God and not all teachers who speak in His name are true disciples themselves. We can know the true way by looking and listening to Jesus. He is the Door and the Gate into the kingdom of God. When we come to Him by faith, believing in Him for the forgiveness of our sins, we enter into the kingdom. True disciples and prophets will point others to Christ as well, rather than to themselves for selfish gain. They will also bear fruit as evidence for their faith.

Apply

Skim through the fruits you listed on Question 9. Are these increasingly evident in your life? Where is the Lord wanting to grow you but you've been resistant to following Him?

Are there any influences on your life that could be characterized by the fruits of the false teacher listed above? If so, who or what are they? By following their lead, what fruits are being produced in your own life?

WRAP-UP: *Session Four*

Jesus lays bare our choice, and in doing so, He invites us to life. What He's asking of us can easily become overwhelming and seem impossible. We must remember that our King goes before us and lives within us. He is the One who produces fruit in and through us. He's the One who, by the Holy Spirit, leads us to righteousness and enables us to obey Him. Again, He is a King who gives. We follow His lead. As Jesus Himself said to us this week, "Ask ... seek ... knock, and it will be opened to you" (Matt. 7:7).

What's one main takeaway you learned about the King and the kingdom this week?

How does knowing this truth change the way you relate to God and others?

WATCH THE SESSION FIVE VIDEO and take notes below. You can find group discussion questions in the leader guide on page 216.

TO ACCESS THE VIDEO TEACHING SESSIONS, USE THE INSTRUCTIONS IN THE BACK OF YOUR BIBLE STUDY BOOK.

EXPANDING
THE
kingdom

SESSION FIVE

Have you ever developed an affinity for something because a good friend's passion about that particular thing or place sparked your own interest? My husband and I have some dear couple friends who attended Penn State so, although we've never been to State College, we perk up when the score of the Penn State football game scrolls by on the TV on Saturdays in the fall. We have an affinity for Penn State and cheer for them to win, because we love people who love the place.

We tend to internalize the likes and dislikes of those closest to us. We love what makes them happy, even if we don't fully share in their affections. We may even take on their mannerisms, word choices, and perspectives over time.

In the past few weeks, we've climbed the mountain with the disciples and listened as Jesus taught them about the culture of the kingdom of God and how, as kingdom citizens, they're called to emulate and obey the King. The disciples didn't just listen to a sermon, however. They also lived and traveled with Jesus throughout His ministry, observing Him act on His teaching authority by healing and extending mercy to those He came in contact with. Living alongside Jesus in every aspect of His days—from rest to ministry to meals—allowed them to internalize who Jesus was and what He cared about. They came to know and embrace in depth His message and His mission. They began to see life through His kingdom's lens, to love what He loved, and to hate what He hated. From this small circle of men, Jesus would change the world for generations to come and extend an invitation into the kingdom to all nations.

Jesus staked His fruitfulness on intentional, relational investment in these few men. The expansion of the kingdom happened through intense discipleship. But true discipleship is truth that is both applied and practiced. Therefore, as Jesus moved closer to the cross, He called for His disciples to take a more active leadership role in His ministry—applying, teaching, and practicing what He taught them. Jesus' discipleship falls into a certain pattern: Jesus does, the disciples observe. Jesus does, the disciples help. The disciples do, Jesus helps them. The disciples do, others observe.[20]

This week, we'll move into the parts of the pattern where Jesus does and the disciples help. Then the disciples are sent out and, when they return, Jesus helps them process what they've seen and done. Jesus is training the disciples, preparing them for the last part of the pattern of ministry after He's gone: The disciples do, someone else watches, and so on. He's preparing them to multiply themselves. Because we're His disciples as well, we have much to learn.

Day One

THE KING'S COMPASSION

Wouldn't you have loved to be among those who walked with Jesus, hearing His sermons and watching Him interact with people? If you could go back in time, what specific moment from Jesus' life would you choose to observe? I personally would choose to observe Him with those the religious leaders considered the greatest sinners and outcasts: the prostitutes, the tax collectors, and the lepers. I can read His words to them in Scripture, but I would give anything to observe His *demeanor* toward them. What did His eyes express? What emotion did He convey? Did He touch them with gentle affection? I'd choose these moments, because I imagine His demeanor would help me know His heart.

We can't go back in time in order to experience these moments, but today's passage provides us the perfect opportunity to consider Jesus' heart for sinners.

In between Jesus preaching the Sermon on the Mount and today's passage, Matthew tells us of many that Jesus healed, including a leper, a centurion's servant, Peter's mother-in-law, a paralytic, blind and mute men, and two who were demon-possessed. He even raised a little girl from the dead. And, as we might expect, "the report of this went through all that district" (Matt. 9:26). Jesus was becoming well-known.

Let's pick up our study in Matthew 9, immediately after these miraculous healings.

READ MATTHEW 9:35.

1) In the verse below, circle the words that indicate the ministry Jesus did and the number of places where Jesus did this ministry.

> And Jesus went throughout all the cities and villages,
> teaching in their synagogues and proclaiming the gospel
> of the kingdom and healing every disease and every affliction.

2) Where did Jesus teach? What does this tell us about who His primary audience has been so far?

3) Gospel means "good news." Based upon what we've studied so far in previous weeks, what is the good news that Jesus proclaimed?

4) If you were in Jesus' audience, how might His actions persuade you regarding His message?

Verse 35 is a closing bookend for an entire section of the Book of Matthew. The front bookend is Matthew 4:23, which is nearly identical to Matthew 9:35. It says, "And he went throughout all Galilee, teaching in their synagogues and proclaiming the gospel of the kingdom and healing every disease and every affliction among the people." And, notably, what sits between these two bookends is the Sermon on the Mount.

By using these two bookends, Matthew indicates two important truths. The first is this: Jesus is teaching with authority and then proving that authority through acts of mercy and healing. He is a King with power and authority, but He is also a King who uses that power and authority for the benefit of people. He is a good and benevolent King.

Matthew's second indication through the second bookend is that we're reaching a pivot point in Jesus' ministry. The disciples had observed Jesus' marvelous works; they had heard Him proclaim kingdom law. And in today's passage, Jesus commissioned them to begin expanding their circle.

IN LIGHT OF THESE TWO TRUTHS, READ MATTHEW 9:36-38.

5) What caused the crowds to gather around Jesus?

- Matthew 4:24-25:

- Matthew 7:28–8:1:

- Matthew 9:27-31:

- Matthew 9:32-34:

What, then, seems to be their intention in coming to Him?

6) How did Jesus feel about the people in these crowds? What does this tell you about who Jesus is?

7) Why did He feel this way about them?

8) Using a dictionary, write the definition of *harassed* below. Who or what were the crowds harassed by?

9) Using a dictionary, write the definition of *helpless* below. What were the crowds helpless to do?

Jesus used two metaphors to help the disciples understand how He saw the crowd before Him. The first metaphor was given by the disciple Matthew; it's not quoted directly from Jesus, as is the second metaphor. Perhaps we can assume it's an illustration Matthew heard Jesus use, or perhaps Matthew attempted to describe the type and amount of compassion he saw in Jesus as He moved among the crowds of people. Nevertheless, both are relatable metaphors to the agricultural context of the region.

As Jesus looked at the crowds, He first saw sheep without a shepherd.

10) In order to understand what He meant, read Numbers 27:15-17 and Ezekiel 34:1-6, and make observations about who the sheep are, who the shepherds are, and what characterizes each.

SHEEP	SHEPHERDS
Who are they?	Who are they?
What characterizes them?	What characterizes them?

11) On Day Five of Week Four, we learned that Jesus described Himself as a door or gate opening into God's kingdom. Looking at John 10:7-11, answer the following questions:

• Who specifically did Jesus say He is a gate or entrance for?

• Aside from being the door or gate, how else did He describe Himself?

• Is it only Israel that Jesus described as the lost sheep He longs to shepherd? (See Isa. 53:6a.)

Sheep are helpless animals. If they fall onto their backs, they cannot right themselves. They also instinctively follow the leader, whether it be another sheep or a shepherd, which is why a good shepherd is vitally important to their well-being. A good shepherd remains highly alert to the safety and care of his or her sheep and leads them to pastures suited for grazing. So when Jesus looked at the crowds, He had compassion on them, because He longed to bring them into peace and life. He longed to bring them with Him into God's kingdom.

12) As Jesus looked at the crowds, the second thing He saw was a field full of healthy crops at harvest time. Combining this metaphor with the first, what was Jesus saying to His disciples?

13) According to Jesus, what was the problem? What did Jesus want His disciples to do in response to the problem? Does this seem odd or inconsequential to you after reading about the vast needs of the lost sheep? Why do you think Jesus commanded His disciples to pray rather than take other actions?

Jesus gave His disciples His eyes and perspective for people: they were sheep following other aimless sheep; they were in danger of being preyed upon; and they were desperately looking for the peace and security of being cared for by a good shepherd.

Apply

We also are surrounded by crowds: neighbors, family members, friends, and coworkers. When you interact with people who don't know Jesus and are wandering aimlessly through life as a sheep without a shepherd, do you look at them with compassion or contempt? How does Jesus' perspective and His use of these two metaphors alter your perspective?

Jesus told the disciples to pray for laborers who will engage with His lost sheep. Pray for two specific people who come to mind. Pray for laborers to engage them. Pray that God would give you an opportunity to tell them about the gate and pasture you've found.

READ PSALM 100.

Psalm 100 is a song of joy at entering through God's gate and being cared for by Him. Name specific ways your Good Shepherd has provided for you and led you to safety. Do as the psalmist said: give thanks to God today.

Day Two

THE KING'S COMMISSION

When friends ask you to join them in praying for their needs or desires, what often happens in your heart as you earnestly pray for them? Praying for our friends (and, as Scripture commands, our enemies) naturally encourages us to put ourselves in the shoes of another. As we consider what to pray, we imagine what they're experiencing, what they might feel, and what we'd desire if we were in their situation. Our empathy and compassion for them expand, as well as our desire to engage in their lives in helpful and appropriate ways. Through prayer, God gives us eyes to see what He wants to do in the world around us. He also implants specific passions in us and compels us toward service through prayer. In other words, in conversation with Him, He gives us His heart. And His is a sending, outwardly-engaging, loving heart. His love is a dynamic, compelling love that sends us toward others.

This is the transition we'll see in today's study. As Jesus looked over the crowds forming around Him, He asked the disciples to pray for laborers to reach them. He knew prayer would expand their compassion for others and prepare them to joyfully participate in His mission and ministry.

1) Read Matthew 10:1-4. Who were Jesus' disciples, and what do we learn about them (vv. 2-4)? (The blue boxes will remain blank.)

DISCIPLE'S NAME	DESCRIPTOR GIVEN

2) What else have we already learned about some of these men? (See Matt. 4:18-22.)

3) Simon is called a Zealot. What is a Zealot? Using a dictionary, write a definition below.

4) What two actions did Jesus take in relation to His disciples (v. 1)? What of His was He sharing with them?

In verse 2, the disciples were called apostles for the first time. Luke 6:13 gives further clarification that these Twelve were chosen out of a larger group of disciples and named apostles. While disciples were any of those who followed and believed in Jesus, apostles were a select group of men who were Jesus' representatives and kingdom ambassadors and given unique authority and specific tasks.

5) We've just seen how Jesus shared with the apostles His authority over unclean spirits and diseases. According to Mark 3:14, what was the specific task they were being sent out to do?

The apostles had everything they needed to go out as ambassadors of the kingdom. They had internalized the message of the kingdom and the compassion of the King. They had observed how Jesus acted on His compassion through His ministry of mercy. God sent the Son in love, and now the Son was sending them forth in love, to do for others just as He had done for them.

6) Although Luke may have combined the commissioning of the apostles with the commissioning of a greater number of people, how does Luke 10:1 describe the manner in which Jesus sends them? (Also note how Matthew lists the names of the apostles in 10:2-4.) What important principle does this teach us about serving as ambassadors of the kingdom of God?

READ MATTHEW 10:5-15 TO DISCOVER WHAT JESUS SAID TO THE APOSTLES BEFORE SENDING THEM OUT AS KINGDOM AMBASSADORS.

7) What group of people did Jesus want the apostles to focus their ministry on? Where have we seen this language before? (See Matt. 9:36.)

8) What groups were they not to focus their ministry on? To understand this restriction, look up the following passages and record your insights:

• Acts 3:25-26:

• Acts 13:46-47:

• Romans 1:16:

9) Returning to Matthew 10:5-15, what did Jesus say the apostles' five main tasks should be?

1.
2.
3.
4.
5.

In fulfilling these tasks, who would the apostles directly emulate word-for-word and action-for-action?

10) In verse 8, Jesus spoke to their motivation for ministering to the lost sheep of Israel. What do you think He meant when He said, "You received without paying; give without pay"? What had the apostles received that they were now to give?

11) Next, Jesus detailed *how* they were to go about fulfilling their five main tasks. Fill in the chart based upon what He said in verses 9-14.

WHAT THE APOSTLES WERE TO DO	WHAT THE APOSTLES WERE NOT TO DO

12) Who did Jesus consider a "worthy" person? Read verses 11-14 in the Amplified Bible to help with your understanding.

13) Jesus described two responses the apostles would encounter: acceptance and rejection. What does this tell us about being an ambassador of the kingdom? Why do you think Jesus told them about these responses in advance?

14) When a person rejects a kingdom ambassador, what did Jesus say they are ultimately rejecting? (Hint: Look again at verses 11-14 in the Amplified Bible.)

Jesus told the apostles not to pack extra food or clothing, indicating that He was sending them on a relatively short mission. We get the sense of apprenticeship: the apostles were stepping out to take on the role they had seen Jesus alone play up to this point. Jesus called them into a leadership position rather than an observant, spectator position. This was the "disciples do, Jesus helps" part of their discipleship. He was already preparing them for when He would leave them after the resurrection and task them to go into all the world and make disciples of all nations (Matt. 28:19).

As the apostle Paul said, "We are ambassadors for Christ, God making his appeal through us" (2 Cor. 5:20). Ambassadors are authorized messengers, sent to a foreign country as representatives for their homeland. Therefore, as kingdom ambassadors who know we're loved by God, we're compelled by that love to declare it to others. This is the kingdom commission.

Apply

Where has God specifically placed you to be an ambassador for His kingdom? (Think relationships, vocation, neighborhood, etc.)

When we become aware of a need or notice a lack of ministry in a certain area of the church or community, that may be an indication that God is calling us to get involved. What unmet need do you see in your church or community that concerns you? Do you sense God "sending you out" in some way?

Are you declaring the good news that Jesus came to save sinners and making an appeal for others to come into the kingdom? Look for an opportunity to share the gospel this week, prepare for the opportunity in prayer, and then make your appeal.

THE KING'S PREDICTION

When I was a teenager, the last thing I wanted to hear was advice from my parents. I assumed our generational differences were so vast that they couldn't possibly understand or help with my experiences and decisions in dating, academics, or friendship. The truth was that their advice was often almost prophetic in nature. They could rightly predict the outcome of a situation, because they'd developed wisdom through lived experiences I didn't yet have.

Now, of course, I try to explain to my own teenage boys why they should listen to their dad and me, and it's their generation's turn to learn the hard way that parents know a thing or two about life. Like my parents before me, I try to explain how things will go if they choose certain paths. I don't predict because I want to be right; I predict because I want to prepare them to choose what's right when they're faced with challenges.

Jesus didn't just send His apostles to proclaim the kingdom; He prepared them in advance for what they would experience and what obstacles they would encounter. This was an important component in their discipleship, and Jesus told them how they should respond when—not if—the challenges arose.

As we'll discover today, all kingdom ambassadors will at some point face these same challenges. As kingdom ambassadors, we have much to learn from what Jesus tells His apostles.

READ MATTHEW 10:16-25.

1) How did Jesus say the disciples should think of themselves as they went about their task of proclaiming the kingdom to the lost (v. 16)? What did this language communicate to the apostles?

2) Jesus told them to navigate the danger of being attacked and devoured in two ways. What were they (v. 16)?
1.
2.

The NIV replaces "wise" with "shrewd." In ancient Eastern cultures, the serpent was a symbol for shrewdness.[21]

Using a dictionary, write a definition for *shrewd* below.

When we hear the word *serpent* in a biblical context, our minds may immediately go to Genesis 3:1: "Now the serpent was more crafty than any other beast of the field that the LORD God had made." There is an evil intent to the serpent's shrewdness—he is cunning and manipulative. Here, however, Jesus used the idea of the shrewd serpent in a positive light, because the apostles were to combine caution, astuteness, and wisdom with innocence rather than evil. This innocence is symbolized by the dove, a bird that in biblical times represented virtue.

3) What does the Bible teach that we're to be wise and innocent in? Read Romans 16:19 and record your insights below.

4) In Matthew 10:16-25, what did Jesus predict would happen to the apostles? What arenas of community life would this encompass?

5) What was the reason Jesus said these things would happen (v. 18)?

In verse 18, Jesus introduced the Gentiles as an audience the apostles would at some point address. Although this is a change from what He said in verses 5-6, Jesus was giving the apostles a vision of their future—eventually they would take the gospel of the kingdom into extended concentric circles, just as Jesus said to them in Acts 1:8b: "You will be my witnesses in Jerusalem and in all Judea and Samaria, and to the end of the earth."

All of this talk about danger and strife must have been incredibly frightening to the apostles. As sheep, they were leaving the safety of their Shepherd to go directly into a pack of wolves. They would experience rejection and hatred. And they would be asked to speak as kingdom ambassadors before hostile audiences.

6) Jesus predicted their future, but He also gave them a command for when the moments of danger and anxiety came. What was the command (v. 19)?

7) According to Jesus, what truth undergirds a lack of anxiety when we're faced with persecution or challenging situations (v. 20)?

The Spirit of the Father is another name for the Holy Spirit, who is God Himself and who indwells every believer. In Scripture, the Holy Spirit is called various names that help us understand who He is and what He does. He's called "the Spirit of truth" (John 14:17), "Helper" (John 14:16), "the Spirit of life" (Rom. 8:2), "the Spirit of grace" (Heb. 10:29), "the Spirit of wisdom" (Eph. 1:17), and "the Spirit of counsel" (Isa. 11:2).

8) Look up the following passages and record what the Holy Spirit does, as well as how this is beneficial to a kingdom ambassador.

PASSAGE	WHAT ROLE DOES THE HOLY SPIRIT PLAY IN THE BELIEVER'S LIFE?	HOW DOES THIS BENEFIT THE KINGDOM AMBASSADOR?
John 14:26		
John 15:26-27		
John 16:8-11		
Romans 15:13		
Ephesians 3:16		

9) In Matthew 10:21-22, Jesus continued His predictions of what the apostles would experience and encounter. We'll go into this more in tomorrow's study, but for now, list the three types of relationships that Jesus said would be torn apart because of the message of the kingdom.

1.

2.

3.

10) What reason did Jesus give for why the apostles would face such opposition (vv. 24-25; Phil. 1:29)?

11) Jesus offered a drink of water to the parched and anxious soul in verse 22, when He said where this journey ends for the kingdom ambassador. What is the finish line and reward?

12) Does this imply that the apostles must do this work in order to receive salvation or that true disciples will evidence their faith by enduring to the end? Explain your answer.

The apostles didn't earn their salvation through their works and faithful endurance to the end. Instead, their actions revealed the faith of salvation already implanted in their hearts. Thankfully, the same is true for us. We obey out of hearts that have been saved by God through faith, not to earn our place in God's kingdom family.

For those who follow Jesus and represent His kingdom, the King's prediction is that we will face obstacles, challenges, rejection, persecution, and—for some—martyrdom. Because we're united with Christ, we will receive similar treatment that He did. Thankfully, because our Helper, the Holy Spirit, dwells in us, we never face trials alone.

Apply

Although we will face opposition like Jesus did, there is an exception to our treatment by the world, and this exception is what helps and strengthens us as His sheep as we go into a world of wolves.

READ HEBREWS 12:1-4.

How does looking at and considering our Master and Shepherd, as the writer of Hebrews tells us to do, help us endure rejection and trying circumstances?

How does knowing that the Holy Spirit dwells within you and shepherds you in all things bring you comfort today?

Where is God calling you to represent Him among wolves? How can you cultivate both shrewdness and innocence in your interactions as you proclaim His kingdom?

THE KING'S SWORD

As Jesus prepared to send out His apostles to proclaim the kingdom of God, He told them to expect severe opposition. Certainly, as they listened to the King's prediction of their future, the apostles must have been filled with uncertainty and fear. Thankfully, as we'll see today, Jesus addressed their fears outright, reminding them that some fears deserve careful attention and some do not.

READ MATTHEW 10:26-33.

1) "So have no fear of them," Jesus began, which cues us to consider the context of what's come before.

• Who was the "them" of which He spoke (vv. 17-18)?

• What's the command Jesus gave (vv. 19,26)?

• What is "so" in reference to? In other words, what reason had Jesus already given for why they should not fear or be anxious (vv. 19-20)?

2) Jesus gave the apostles two additional reasons they should not fear those who oppose them. What are they (vv. 26,28)?

3) To what "revealing" and "knowing" was He referring in verse 26? Look up the following verses and record your insights:

• Matthew 12:36-37:

• Acts 17:31:

• Romans 2:16:

• 1 Timothy 5:24-25:

4) According to the verses above, who is doing the revealing, knowing, and judging? And what is the standard by which men and women will be judged?

5) What, then, is a healthy fear, according to verse 28?

6) Using a dictionary, write a definition below for *fear* that best fits the context of what Jesus said our posture must be before God.

7) How is this a different type of fear than the fear of men Jesus described in verse 26?

Jesus didn't figuratively slap the apostles' hands or dismiss their fears as if to say, "Just don't think about the difficult things ahead." He wanted them to consider that life as it's intended under His rule and reign isn't only about the physical and tangible things they can see with their eyes. Jesus told them that their *souls* were required of them, so they should seek first the kingdom. He pointed to what really matters as if to say, "Be attentive here instead."

In regard to our attentiveness, Jesus once again pointed to God as Father. You may recall from our study of Matthew 6:25-34 on Week Four, Day Three that Jesus said God as Father is attentive toward our physical needs. He now adds to our understanding of God's attentiveness toward us (and what He wants us to continually consider).

8) What verses in Matthew 10:26-33 support the following statements?

• God sees all, even what no one else sees.

• God knows each of us personally.

• God values each of us individually.

9) What two commands did Jesus give His apostles?

• Verses 26,28,31:

• Verse 27:

10) For a group of men starting out in a challenging ministry where people would reject and hate them, how do you think attending to the truths Jesus had given them about God the Father helped them not fear man and instead emboldened them to proclaim the gospel? Write your thoughts under each statement below.

• God sees all, even what no one else sees.

• God knows each of us personally.

• God values each of us individually.

Jesus said there's something far worse than persecution: a body and soul in hell. And there's something far better than the acceptance and approval of man: the acceptance and approval of the Father. In the next section of Scripture, He drew a distinctive line and asked the disciples to consider what they would choose and to what they would give their lives. The line is so stark it's almost jarring, but perhaps this serves to highlight the importance of choosing rightly.

READ MATTHEW 10:34-39.

11) How do you explain why someone who is called the "Prince of Peace" (Isa. 9:6b) said He didn't come to bring peace but rather a sword?

12) What types of relationships did Jesus say His "sword" might divide? What's the division based upon?

This is where it gets personal. The wolves among the lost sheep of Israel are one thing, but family? I imagine the disciples didn't quite know what to make of Jesus' words. He was, however, calling them to *total* allegiance, saying that those who choose a divided allegiance aren't "worthy" of Him. You may recall from our study of verses 11-14 that Jesus used this term with the disciples before. A "worthy" person isn't someone who earns value by merit or good works; a worthy person is one who receives and welcomes both the messenger and the gospel of the kingdom.

13) What may be present in a person's life who has *not* pledged total allegiance to King Jesus?

- Verse 37a:

- Verse 37b:

- Verse 38:

What's an example of how someone might love a family member more than Jesus?

14) The cross is an instrument of death. What, then, does it mean that Jesus said those who fully receive and welcome Him will take up their crosses?

If we could summarize what Jesus is saying, it might very well be, "Seek first the kingdom of God and his righteousness, and all these things will be added to you" (Matt. 6:33). A worthy person fully embraces Jesus and His message and is willing to endure loss and persecution in order to gain Him. A worthy person sets her heart and mind on the kingdom to come and her place in that kingdom, rather than on an earthly and temporary kingdom.

This is a person who knows the love and constant companionship of God the Father, who knows that He gives far more to us than He asks of us, and who knows that Jesus' call to allegiance is an invitation to true peace and joy.

Apply

How do the truths about God given in today's study speak to you in what you're currently encountering in your relationships, work, and ministry?

What's an example of an unhealthy fear of man you're struggling to resist? How is this divided allegiance affecting your peace and joy? How can you replace this fear with a holy fear of God?

When have you known that following Jesus means you must take up your cross in a specific area of your life? What did you choose? What was the outcome?

THE KING'S REWARD

Our idea of following and serving Jesus—our idea of the blessed life, for that matter—doesn't always align with what Jesus has told His followers. How could what is right and true be so costly and difficult? In response, Jesus continually calls us to look forward and to remember that this earthly kingdom is quickly passing away. There is full, eternal life ahead, and in the kingdom of God, everything done in Jesus' name is seen and will be rewarded.

As Jesus sent His disciples out among the wolves, His parting words to them centered around this theme: cost and reward.

READ MATTHEW 10:40-42.

1) Label who Jesus referred to with each pronoun in verse 40.

Whoever receives *you* _____

Receives *me* _____

Whoever receives *me* _____

Receives *him* who sent me _____

Jesus said to His disciples that just as He was intimately connected to and identified with His Father, they were intimately connected to and identified with both King Jesus and God the Father. There was no distinction; they couldn't be separated out. They were united with Christ, enveloped within the love, protection, attributes, and power of the triune God.

We, too, as followers of Jesus are united with Him. While living temporarily in the earthly kingdom, this comes with cost. We've seen this laid out clearly in our study of Matthew 10.

2) Fill in the chart below with what Jesus said His disciples would encounter because they were identified and united with Him.

VERSE(S)	WHAT DID BEING IDENTIFIED WITH CHRIST MEAN FOR OR COST THE DISCIPLES?
Matthew 10:17-18	
Matthew 10:22	

VERSE(S)	WHAT DID BEING IDENTIFIED WITH CHRIST MEAN FOR OR COST THE DISCIPLES?
Matthew 10:24-25	
Matthew 10:39	

How some people have responded to Jesus—with doubt, skepticism, anger, and wariness—is how they will respond to those identified with Him. What Jesus faces—the cross—is what the disciples face in some lesser form.

However, there is a reward that far outweighs the cost for those who are united with Christ. In this life, there is both cost and reward. But in the kingdom to come, there is only reward, no cost. And in this reward, we will live eternally with our King.

3) In Matthew 10, Jesus sprinkled details about the rewards for those who follow Him. Fill in the chart below with these details.

VERSE(S)	WHAT DID THE DISCIPLES GAIN FROM BEING UNITED WITH CHRIST?
Matthew 10:20	
Matthew 10:22	
Matthew 10:26	
Matthew 10:32-33	
Matthew 10:39	

In no uncertain terms, Jesus told the disciples that what was His was also theirs. And because they were willing to endure the costs that pledging allegiance to Him meant, He would proclaim each of them as His before the Father He loves (v. 32). He would name and acknowledge what they did in His name and what they would endure because of Him. He would express in words what was already true: each one of His followers was intimately tied to Him.

Just think of it: as followers of Jesus, we'll one day hear of His undying love for us as He speaks it before the Father!

4) The theme of being united with Christ and gaining from His cost is all over the New Testament. Look up the following verses and record what gains are ours because of Him.

VERSE(S)	WHAT GAIN IS OURS BECAUSE WE'RE IN CHRIST?
John 17:23	
Romans 6:5	
Romans 8:1	
2 Corinthians 5:21	
Galatians 2:20	
Ephesians 2:1-7	

5) Aside from the apostles, who also receives a reward, according to Matthew 10:41-42?

There are costs to following and serving Jesus, because there were costs for Him in coming to earth and proclaiming the kingdom, and we're identified with Him. But because He endured the cross, the cost of His life is what brought many sons and daughters to glory (Heb. 2:10) and what enables us to walk in freedom from condemnation and wholeheartedly live for Him. We're loved and approved of by God the Father because we're identified with the Son. This sets the costs of a godly life in perspective, as well as great joy in our hearts.

Apply

Of the gains you discovered in Question 4, which most resonates with you? What might change in your life if you meditated consistently on your union with Christ and what He's won you?

If you are in Christ, one day Jesus will acknowledge you before God the Father. God the Father will receive you as He receives His very Son. How does imagining that day help you face the current challenges in your life?

WRAP-UP: *Session Five*

This week, we've seen how Jesus' ministry took a sharp turn. He handed some of His ministry and authority to His disciples and sent them out in order to expand the kingdom of God. Before they went, He told them what they should expect: some would receive their message and others would reject it. They were warned and prepared in advance, armed with the truth that rejection is not personal but is a rejection of Christ Himself. At the same time, we learned that rewards await the faithful disciple of Christ for the same reason rejection awaits him or her: because we're united and identified with Christ our King.

> What's one main takeaway you learned about the King and the kingdom this week?

> How does knowing this truth change the way you relate to God and others?

WATCH THE SESSION SIX VIDEO and take notes below. You can find group discussion questions in the leader guide on page 216.

TO ACCESS THE VIDEO TEACHING SESSIONS, USE THE INSTRUCTIONS IN THE BACK OF YOUR BIBLE STUDY BOOK.

139

CHARACTERISTICS
OF THE
kingdom

SESSION SIX

I'm fascinated by productive gardens and beautifully arranged potted plants and have always wanted to learn how to begin and cultivate my own green, flowering beauties. For my birthday this year, my husband gave me the best gift I've ever received: he gifted me a horticulturist's skills. The horticulturist—a friend of ours—came to our home and taught me how to arrange and pot plants for our back porch, how to water and feed them (read: keep them alive), and how to nurture and prune them over time. The horticulturist's primary refrain was perseverance: each day, he said, I should give the plants proper attention, and over time I'd not only become a full-fledged plant lady, but I'd also enjoy beautiful flowers on our back deck no matter the season.

In the Gospel of Matthew, Jesus used many agricultural word pictures to describe the kingdom of God. This should tell us something—that the kingdom of God is to be nurtured, cultivated, and may involve pruning. It's also continually growing and producing fruit, but this growth may happen in subtle, imperceptible ways, like a seed tucked away underground.

As kingdom citizens, perseverance must become a theme and goal of our lives.

Last week we saw that, as Jesus sent the disciples out in pairs to emulate His own ministry of truth and mercy, He commissioned them with words of caution and promise of reward. He predicted the obstacles and challenges they would face in their mission, and we learned that these are the same obstacles and challenges we face as kingdom citizens today. The good news is that, because we're identified with Christ, we enjoy the love, provision, and help of God the Father. He goes with us wherever we go, enabling us to live godly lives and serve Him.

This week, Jesus digs deeper into this theme: it is God's kingdom and, ultimately, He is the one working to build it. Though we're commissioned into the work and though the way is narrow and steep, we go in His name, by His power, resting under His protection and provision. We, then, must develop *perseverance* in our kingdom work and as we wait for the full realization of a kingdom we can't yet see and experience. We must understand how the kingdom works: it's constructed slowly and often in unseen ways. And, most of all, we must understand God's role in the kingdom so we can also better understand ours.

This is where Jesus took His disciples, as recorded in Matthew 13, and it's where we'll be this week, listening in as Jesus used parables—many of them agriculturally themed—to describe the characteristics of the kingdom of God.

Day One

THE KINGDOM IS LIKE
A SOWER SOWING SEED

In a sermon many years ago, my husband Kyle used an illustration to communicate a biblical truth, as he often does. Unfortunately, he used a story about my inability to perfect a pecan pie (his favorite dessert) as the illustration. (He's since learned to ask for permission if an illustration involves me—especially one that highlights my foibles!) That particular Sunday, I was serving in the nursery, and as parents came to pick up their children, I became deeply confused as to why so many were offering me their favorite pecan pie recipe. After a few of these offers, it dawned on me that Kyle had probably said something about my recent attempts at baking in the sermon, and if there is anything congregants remember, it's always the illustration.

We're all drawn to illustrations and stories that help us grasp intangible truths. There's something about being able to mentally picture what's being communicated that not only helps us understand it but also stirs our emotions, creating a deeper, more memorable imprint.

The kingdom of God is an intangible reality that is difficult to grasp. This week, we'll see that Jesus understood His disciples' difficulty and chose to communicate with them through the use of tangible illustrations.

When we last encountered Jesus in Matthew 10, His apostles were leaving His side to go to "the lost sheep of the house of Israel" with the good news that the kingdom of God was at hand. In between Matthew 10 and our text for today, Matthew records how Jesus continued teaching and preaching in various cities, answered John the Baptist's question about whether or not He was the Messiah, and answered inquiries from the scribes and Pharisees about everything from healing on the Sabbath to signs and wonders. At some point—it's not specifically detailed by Matthew—the disciples returned from their mission to Jesus' side, and He continued to teach them about the kingdom.

READ MATTHEW 13:1-23.

1) Matthew set the scene in verses 1-2. Record the details he gave.

• Where did this scene take place?

- From where did Jesus speak? Why?

- From what we've learned previously, what's the significance of Jesus being seated as He teaches?

- Aside from the crowd, who else was on the scene? (See also v. 10.)

2) Jesus' teaching in this section is different from the Sermon on the Mount in one significant way. What new rhetorical device did Jesus utilize in His teaching (v. 3)?

3) A parable is an allegorical story designed to illustrate or teach a truth. Using a dictionary, write the definition of *allegory* below.

4) Jesus used concrete, tangible examples from everyday life in order to help His audience grasp intangible, unseen realities about the kingdom of God. What reason did Jesus give for why He taught through parables (vv. 11,13)?

What connection did the writer Matthew make with Jesus' use of parables? (See vv. 34-35.)

Let's explore Matthew 13:10-17 in detail in order to understand what Jesus meant when He said to His disciples, "To you it has been given to know the secrets of the kingdom of heaven, but to them it has not been given" (v. 11). This understanding will help us as we study the parables this week and in the coming weeks.

5) READ MATTHEW 13:11.

- Who was the "you" to which Jesus referred?

- Who was the "them" (v. 2)?

- What did Mark 4:11 call "them"? What made this group distinct from the disciples?

6) What do you think Jesus meant by "the secrets of the kingdom of heaven" (v. 11)? (See Matt. 11:25; Eph. 3:1-6; and Col. 1:25-27 for help.)

The crowds heard Jesus' words, but they didn't understand what He was saying. However, it wasn't just that they didn't understand; it's that they *didn't want* to understand. By referencing Isaiah 6:9-10, a passage that tells of the way people stubbornly refused to accept Isaiah's proclamations about God, Jesus was saying the crowds in His day were similarly at fault. They didn't desire the truth.

The disciples, on the other hand, had seen and believed, heard and understood—a gift from God, in that He had opened up their spiritual eyes and given them sight. They believed Jesus was the Messiah, and upon this truth each disciple would grow or, as Jesus said, "he will have an abundance" (Matt. 13:12).

Allegiance and submission to Jesus as King is the seed of the kingdom that, when implanted by the Holy Spirit, causes one's spiritual life and understanding to grow. We begin to understand with spiritual eyes what we can't see with physical ones.

Now let's look at the specific parable with which Jesus begins His teaching—often called the parable of the sower—and discover what truth about the kingdom of God He's conveying to those who follow Him.

REREAD MATTHEW 13:3-9.

7) Although he isn't named, what was the role of the main character in this parable about the kingdom of God?

8) Fill in the chart below with the details Jesus gave about the seeds and what happens to them.

SEEDS/VERSE	LOCATION OF THE SEED	WHAT BECAME OF THE SEED?
Seed #1 (v. 4)		
Seed #2 (vv. 5-6)		
Seed #3 (v. 7)		
Seed #4 (v. 8)		

Jesus concluded the parable by saying, "He who has ears, let him hear" (v. 9). He was saying to the crowd that they shouldn't just *hear* the words but seek to *understand* the words. There is a spiritual truth about the kingdom of God hidden in the allegory.

Thankfully for us, when Jesus was alone with His disciples, He explained the spiritual truth He taught the crowds through the parable.

REREAD MATTHEW 13:18-23.

9) Let's identify the various components of the parable.

• What was the seed that was being sown (v. 19)?

• What were people—the hearers—identified as in the story? In other words, to what concrete and tangible object did Jesus equate our hearts?

• Jesus never directly identified who the sower was, but based upon how we've identified the seed and the soil, who did the sower represent in the parable?

10) Fill in the chart below with Jesus' explanation about His parable.

SEEDS/VERSE	Location of the Seed	What sort of person was described? What was their relationship to the seed?	What was this person's outcome?
Seed #1 (v. 19)	Along the path		
Seed #2 (vv. 20-21)	Rocky ground		
Seed #3 (v. 22)	Among thorns		
Seed #4 (v. 23)	Good soil		

11) Jesus cautioned against a lack of endurance. What specifically accounted for the second seed/person's lack of endurance? (See Luke 8:13.)

12) Not all who face testing or tribulation fall away and become unfruitful, but Jesus said one who "has no root in himself" (Matt. 13:21) is in danger of not grasping God's kingdom. What do you think He meant by that?

Jesus also cautioned against becoming entangled in the cares of the world and the deceitfulness of riches and, therefore, unfruitful. Both the cares of this world and the worries of life take us away from the truth of Jesus and our place in His kingdom. When we do this, we choose a different discipleship, a different master, and we become choked by our divided mind.

13) Finally, Jesus commended those who are "good soil." What makes for good soil, according to verse 23, and how is this person distinct from the ones before?

Jesus said that, for the one whose heart is submitted under the authority of God through obedience to His Word, the fruit will be thirtyfold, sixtyfold, hundredfold. In that time, average agricultural yields ranged from fivefold to fifteenfold, which was considered a good crop.[22] In Genesis 26:12, it was said that Isaac's crop was hundredfold, and this was God's blessing on his life. Jesus was saying here that God flourishes the person who submits to His good rule and to His Word.

The crop the disciple bears is one of love, joy, peace, patience, goodness, kindness, faithfulness, and self-control. Psalm 1:3 describes this person as a tree planted by streams of water that yields fruit in its season and whose leaf does not wither. This person has true life. This person is sturdy, strong, not easily carried away by the destructive and death-giving desires of self or the world. This is a person who is flourishing. It's a promise that, as we receive with a submissive heart, placing ourselves under the living Word of God, we *will* grow in faith, love, hope, and joy. For this is the way the kingdom works.

We're receivers, receptacles for the seed Jesus sows. According to the parable, we can receive His words in various ways, but only one way of receiving yields a seed-bearing plant that grows up strong and withstands the elements. The primary way we receive the words of Jesus today is through the Bible, as the Holy Spirit illuminates it to us, teaches us, and helps us understand it.

Apply

We're all being discipled. Whatever we input into our minds is discipling us, whether it's our own self-condemning thoughts that we rehearse over and over, what we watch and listen to, or who we emulate and listen to. What or who are you being primarily discipled by? Does Jesus indicate this will be fruitful for you?

What cares of the world or deceitfulness of riches are choking out your desire for the Word of God? What do you need to ask God to root out in order to make your heart "good soil" for His Word?

Day Two

THE KINGDOM IS LIKE A FIELD BEFORE HARVEST

My sister and brother-in-law farm thousands of acres of land in south Texas. They grow various crops, but their primary crop is cotton. When the crop shows itself ready, my brother-in-law and their hired workers labor as many hours as they can manage, even after dark, to get the cotton out of the ground. But they must wait and watch the crop for its telltale signs: the cotton boll turns soft green, then hardens and starts to speckle and turn brown before it eventually cracks and opens. The boll then reveals its white fiber, and the fields look like they're dotted with white, puffy clouds. Harvest can begin.

Yesterday we learned that the kingdom of God is like a sower sowing the seed of the kingdom into hearts. That seed, when received and obeyed in "good soil," grows into a healthy crop and reproduces itself. Today, through the use of another parable, Jesus helps His listeners—both the crowds and the disciples—build upon their understanding of what the kingdom of God is like. He will ask us to take on the perspective of a farmer looking out across his fields in order to help His audience grasp intangible, unseen realities about the kingdom.

1) Read Matthew 13:24-30,36-43. To what tangible picture does Jesus again compare the intangible kingdom of God (v. 24)?

In the parable of the sower, the enemy of the kingdom is characterized as a bird that snatches away the good seed the Sower has sown.

2) What additional detail do we learn in verse 25 about how the enemy of the kingdom works?

The enemy sowed *zizanion* ("weeds") among the master's field, which most commentators think is bearded darnel, a close cousin to wheat and difficult to distinguish from each other when the plants are young. Only when the heads of grain appear on the wheat can they be distinguished. In addition, the roots of the two plants, when sown in the same field, entangle themselves together below ground,[23] so any attempt to separate them before harvest endangers the wheat crop while it's growing to maturity.

3) Using verses 36-43, identify four of the characters and objects of your choosing from the story and examine them more closely in the chart below.

CONCRETE OBJECT OR CHARACTER	WHAT OR WHO IT REPRESENTS IN THE KINGDOM OF GOD

The master of the house did the sowing in the field, which seems unusual considering he has many servants at his disposal. Notably, while in the previous parable people are characterized as soil, in this parable, people are the seed itself and also the servants working in the field.

4) What does this teach us about God's role and responsibility in the kingdom of God? Our role and responsibility in the kingdom of God?

5) Who do you think the servants represent in the parable?

6) What two questions did the servants ask the master of the house? Write them in your own words below.

• Verse 27:

• Verse 28:

7) The servants noticed both wheat and darnel growing together. What does this tell us about which agricultural stage the field was in? What was soon to come?

8) Jesus used the symbolic questions as a means of teaching truths about Himself (the Master and Sower) and how the kingdom works. What was He trying to convey in His rhetorical questions and answers?

Jesus used this parable to teach that this earthly kingdom is much like a field just before harvest, and that the fully realized kingdom of God will be inaugurated by a reaping and a separating. Only one of those separated crops will be brought in by the Master—the wheat, or the sons of the kingdom. The sons of the enemy—the law-breakers—won't be brought in by the Master, but they'll instead be separated from Him forever.

Jesus ended His parable with the familiar phrase: "He who has ears, let him hear" (v. 43). He was cautioning the crowds to seek understanding, to prepare for the eventual harvest by receiving the good seed of the kingdom and letting that seed produce a good crop within them.

For the disciples, and for all who follow Jesus, this parable serves as a comfort. In an earthly kingdom where the wicked seem to thrive unchecked and where the righteous cry out, "How long, O Lord?," we hear our Master say all will be dealt with justly in the end. Although the kingdom is at hand—Jesus has come—there's a delay to the consummated kingdom's arrival. Eventually, we'll be brought in by the Master at harvest time, but we currently can't see the full reality of what God is doing. This is where Jesus turns our attention next.

READ MATTHEW 13:31-33.

9) Jesus used two more concrete objects to help us understand what the kingdom of God is like and how it works. Fill in the chart below according to His explanation.

	VERSES 31-32	VERSE 33
The kingdom of God is like …		
How did Jesus describe this object? Or what do you know about this object?		

	VERSES 31-32	VERSE 33
What became of the object?		
What does this teach us about the way the kingdom works?		

The kingdom of God is somewhat hidden for now, because it is the rule and reign of Jesus Christ in the hearts of men and women. It does show itself over time, however, because the Sower produces life and fruit that can be seen outwardly, and He turns His disciples into places of refuge for others.

10) What is the end for those who follow Jesus (v. 43; Prov. 4:18-19)?

As kingdom citizens, we can't see the kingdom of God with our eyes yet. But Jesus paints us a picture, telling us that the kingdom is like a field just before harvest. In other words, the kingdom is coming, and we must not give up as we wait for its arrival.

Apply

In the waiting and longing, how do you tend to question God's will and ways as the servants questioned their master? How does Jesus' parable instruct and/or comfort you?

As we'll see in our further study of Jesus' parables, He primarily characterizes us as, first, servants working in the master's field or house and, second, as children. Do you most often think of yourself as a servant and child or do you think of yourself as master and leader of your own life? How does Jesus identifying you as servant and child give you perspective on your roles and responsibilities within the kingdom?

Day Three

THE KINGDOM IS LIKE HIDDEN TREASURE

As we begin today, let's revisit our working definition of the kingdom of heaven (or kingdom of God). The kingdom of heaven is a *people* who enjoy God's *provision* and rest under His *protective power* in a specific *place*.

Because the kingdom of God is partially "hidden" for now, Jesus uses concrete examples, or parables, to help His listeners grasp what they can't yet see. So far, He's explained that the kingdom is like a farmer sowing seed and those that gladly receive and obey His message become fruitful and life-bearing. He's also described the kingdom as a field just before harvest, healthy wheat mixed with darnel that will be separated after the crop is brought in. In our study today, Jesus will share four more parables in quick succession to describe what the kingdom is like.

1) BEFORE WE BEGIN, LET'S SET THE SCENE. READ MATTHEW 13:36-38.

- Where did this scene take place?

- Who was Jesus teaching?

- From where did Jesus and the disciples retreat?

NOW READ MATTHEW 13:44-46.

Jesus tied together two parables with the word "again" in verse 45. In other words, these two parables teach a similar truth about the kingdom. Their pairing expresses emphasis, just as we might repeat a message we want to make sure our listener receives.

2) Fill in the chart below with the details Jesus gave the disciples.

PARABLE	To what was the kingdom compared?	How was the object discovered?	What was the person's response to finding the object?	Why was this the person's response?
13:44				
13:45-46				

3) In both parables, what do you think Jesus was emphasizing? Check what best applies.

☐ The person's work to find the object and the cost to him of gaining that object

☐ The worth of what the person discovered

In both parables, the people don't hesitate to invest *all* they have into obtaining the object they've found. The worth of the kingdom far surpasses all their worldly goods combined.

4) Using the ESV, fill in the blanks from Philippians 3:8-9a:

"I count _____ as loss because of the
_____ _____ of knowing Christ Jesus
my Lord. For his sake I have suffered the loss of _____ things
and count them as rubbish, in order that I may _____ Christ and
be found in him ..."

Like the man and the merchant in the parables Jesus told, Paul used all-encompassing language ("all" and "everything") to show that gaining Christ and His kingdom is worth more than anything else in this life combined.

5) According to Philippians 3:8-11, what did Paul gain in God's kingdom?

6) Returning to Matthew 13, the disciples had already chosen to "leave all" and follow Jesus. They were, in essence, embodying the truths of these parables. What, then, do you think Jesus was communicating to them through these parables?

LET'S MOVE ON TO THE THIRD PARABLE JESUS TOLD HIS DISCIPLES. READ MATTHEW 13:47-50.

7) Jesus used the word "again" to connect this parable with a previous one we've already studied. He was once again pairing two concrete examples to teach and emphasize a similar truth about the kingdom. Which parable from Matthew 13 was He connecting with verses 47-50?

8) In both parables, what do you think Jesus was emphasizing to His disciples?

JESUS CONCLUDED WITH A FOURTH PARABLE. READ MATTHEW 13:51-52 IN THE NIV.

9) In this parable, what had the teacher of the law become?

10) In the kingdom of God, what does the disciple store up and treasure? What do you think is meant by the "old" and the "new"?

11) Matthew, as we established very early in our study, wrote the Gospel of Matthew with the purpose of connecting the Law and the Prophets (the Old Testament) to Jesus as the fulfillment (the New Testament). How does this further your understanding of what Jesus was saying?

In these four parables, Jesus grows His disciples' understanding of the nature of the kingdom. We've learned it is *partially hidden*, like a seed nestled underground, a crop of wheat with roots entangled with darnel, leaven mixed in dough, treasure underground, or a pearl tucked in an oyster. We see signs of the kingdom when we see signs of life and health in the crop, risen bread, or the pearl discovered and harvested. In other words, our external lives evidence the work of God in our hearts.

In addition, we've learned that the kingdom is of *immeasurable value*, far surpassing anything of worldly significance or value and worth our wholehearted devotion.

Apply

Paul, when looking for confidence in himself, looked to his racial, social, and religious pedigree. All of these together, he said, couldn't come close to the worth and value of knowing Christ and being found in Him. What are one or two things aside from Christ that you place confidence in before God or think validate your worth in the eyes of others? What value do these things hold in the kingdom of God?

How does the partially hidden nature of the kingdom both challenge and comfort you?

Day Four

THE KINGDOM IS LIKE
A STEWARDED PROPERTY

Gladys Aylward was a British-born single woman who served as a missionary in China her whole adult life. God called her to missions as a young woman, but being a school dropout and from an impoverished family, Gladys struggled to understand how exactly God might use her. Nonetheless, she served several years as a parlor maid in England, accumulating money to pay for her passage to China. When Gladys finally arrived in China, "she looked around and realized that God had been preparing her for this day since before her birth. Many years later, Gladys told Elisabeth Elliot about two childhood heartaches. One had been that all the other girls had golden curls while she had black hair. The other was that everybody else kept growing while she stopped at four feet, ten inches. Now in [China], she stood in the midst of the people God had prepared her for. They all had black hair, and none of them had kept growing."[24]

Everything we are and have—even short stature—is a gift from God that He can use in the cultivation of His kingdom.

So far this week, Jesus, speaking in parables, has said the kingdom of heaven is like a treasure buried in a field. A man finds the treasure and, exultant in his discovery, sells everything he has in order to buy the field. He releases all his previous holdings and invests his life, future, and well-being in this plot of land. The foundation of his joy is not the land itself but the knowledge of the treasure it contains.

Today we will learn that Jesus didn't expect this man to live out his days sitting on his investment, waiting for the day the treasure was unveiled for all to see. Instead, the treasure causes him to cultivate the land he owns. Joy in finding an invaluable treasure leads to cultivation, and cultivation to further joy. He cultivates life using what he's been gifted, because he's found life.

READ MATTHEW 25:14-30.

1) Let's first identify the main characters and points in the parable.

• What is the "it" in verse 14? (See 25:1.)

- What are we told about the "man" in verses 14-15? Who does the man represent?

- Who do the servants represent? What are the servants given to do?

- What is meant by a "talent"? Use your Bible's notes or a study Bible to discover the answer and write it below. Is a talent a small amount of money or an extravagant amount of money?

- We aren't told specifically in this passage, but Jesus told other parables that may indicate what sort of property the man owns. Look at your Bible's section title for Matthew 20:1-16. What kind of property might this be?

The Greek word for "servants" in this parable is *doulos*, meaning bondservant. A bondservant in biblical times was one who had fully renounced his or her rights and had given themselves in voluntary service to their master. (See also Ex. 21:5-6.)

2) What does Jesus' use of this word (*doulos*) tell us about the relationship between the master and the servants in the parable?

3) The servants were entrusted with the master's property, making them stewards and representatives. Using a dictionary, write the definition of *steward* that best suits the parable in the space below.

4) Fill in the white boxes in the chart below according to Jesus'
explanation of what each servant did with the master's money
and how the master responded when he returned.

SERVANT	How much money was the servant given to steward?	What did the servant do with the money he was given?	What was the servant's explanation for why he did what he did with the money?	Upon returning, how did the master respond to the servant?	What did the servant receive from the master as a result?
Servant #1 (vv. 16, 20-21)					
Servant #2 (vv. 17, 22-23)					
Servant #3 (vv. 18, 24-28,30)					

5) Jesus said the master gave the servants different amounts of money
to steward. Why was this not unfair to the servants?

6) What are examples of "talents" we, as Jesus' disciples and kingdom
representatives, are intended to steward? Look up the following verses
and record your insights.

- 1 Corinthians 6:19-20:

- 1 Corinthians 12:4-7:

- 2 Corinthians 1:3-7:

- 2 Corinthians 5:14-15:

- 2 Corinthians 9:6-7,11:

- Galatians 5:13:

7) In the parable, what did the master want each servant to do with what he had been given?

8) What do you think Jesus meant by "you have been faithful over a little; I will set you over much" (Matt. 25:21)?

9) Let's turn our attention to the third servant. Answer the following questions about him:

- What did Jesus call him in verses 26 and 30?

- Based upon his being sent to the place of outer darkness where there is "weeping and gnashing of teeth" (v. 30), was he a true disciple?

- What was the servant's understanding of the master's nature? Is this an accurate picture of the Master, Jesus?

- What was the servant's driving motivation in relation to the master (v. 25)?

10) Jesus used parables to help us understand spiritual truths. What is the overarching spiritual principle He illustrated with this parable?

We've learned that all belongs to the Master, all comes from the Master's hand, and the Master is inevitably responsible for what happens with His property. He is responsible for providing for all under His dominion. He is responsible for bringing forth the crop in His fields. We, as His servants and stewards, aren't responsible for anything beyond faithful obedience with what He's given us, stemming from wholehearted devotion to our King.

To focus on fruitfulness and outcomes is a frustrating endeavor; to work in faith is all we're asked to do.

This is what it means to do kingdom work—that we're cultivators in the specific plot of land we exist in, with the specific talents we've been given.

Apply

Jesus identified His disciples as bondservants. Do you think of yourself as a servant who stewards what the Master owns? Or do you think of yourself as the owner of what you have and who you are? How does this perspective shape how you live?

What specific "talents" has God given you to steward in this life?

How does a focus on faithfulness rather than fruitfulness help define *success* in the use of your talents?

Day Five

THE KINGDOM IS LIKE THE MASTER OF A VINEYARD

Throughout this week of study, we've learned about the nature of the King and His kingdom. Jesus spread the gospel of the kingdom and invited His followers to participate in similar kingdom work, although we're each given unique gifts and "plots of land" to cultivate.

In our passage today, Jesus continued this line of thought with a new parable, addressing the common issue that arises between us when we recognize we're given varying amounts of "talents"—things like comparison, envy, and ultimately a distrust of God's goodness.

READ MATTHEW 20:1-16.

1) To what is the kingdom of heaven compared?

2) Jesus gave several details to set the scene of the parable. Answer the questions below according to what He told His disciples.

• What did the master of the house do (v. 1)?

• What time of day did the master hire his first laborers (v. 1)?

• What kind of property did the master own (v. 1)?

• What did the master of the house pay his laborers (v. 2)?

• Using your study Bible or Bible's notes as a reference, how much is a denarius?

3) In Jesus' telling, the master continued to hire laborers for his vineyard throughout the workday, which was typically 6 a.m. to 6 p.m. Fill in the chart with the information given.

HOUR	TIME	WAGE
Early morning	6 a.m.	1 Denarius
Third	9 a.m.	
Sixth		
Ninth		
Eleventh		

4) What might we assume about the workers who continued to stand in the marketplace until late afternoon? Place a check next to your answer below.

☐ They were lazy.

☐ They were unqualified for the job.

☐ They were desperate for work.

5) Who does the owner of the vineyard represent in Jesus' parable?

What do we learn about the owner?

• Verse 4:

• Verse 15:

What do we learn about the owner by the fact that he continued offering people work up until the last hour of the workday?

6) Which group of laborers grumble at the master and why (vv. 10-11)?

7) The phrase "Do you begrudge?" in verse 15 literally means "Is your eye evil?" How were the laborers hired at 6 a.m. sinning in their "sight"?

In this story, each person received the same generous wage, no matter the work they had done. Although the laborers tried to make the situation about them, Jesus made the story about the owner—God the Father. He owns all and is generous with what He has. The workers in the vineyard—that's us—benefit from His generosity, and we do well to keep our eyes focused on what He's freely given us. When we look out for own interests, thinking we've somehow earned more or deserve more from God than those around us, we become envious, prideful, judgmental, and merciless toward them. We lose sight of God Himself, because our eyes are on others and what He's chosen to give them.

8) The kingdom of God and its gospel is the great equalizer. No matter our socioeconomic background, good works, sin, race, nationality, age, or gender, what does the Bible say those who are in Christ all have in common and in equal amounts?

• Galatians 3:27-29:

• Ephesians 4:4-6:

In each of these passages, who does the acting and who does the receiving?

9) What does God give believers in various amounts? (See the list you made in yesterday's lesson, Question 6.)

10) Now read John 21:17-22 and answer the following questions.

• Where were Peter's eyes: on Jesus or on John?

- What did Peter do with his situation and John's situation?

- What did Peter want Jesus to do?

- Write below what Jesus said to Peter in response in verse 22.

11) What does the parable in Matthew 20:1-16, combined with the other passages we've read today, teach you about the kingdom of God?

The kingdom of God assumes God's goodness and generosity toward those who follow King Jesus. Often, when we compare our lives with the lives of those around us, we see inequities and judge God to be unfair and not good. But when we look at what God has so freely given to us in Christ—all of which is unearned and wholly undeserved—we see the overabundance of grace and mercy bestowed upon us, and we want that same grace and mercy for others. The kingdom of God centers around a throne of grace. We don't have to worry there's not enough to go around.

Apply

Jesus wanted us to know through this parable that God does not deal with us based upon work or merit but rather upon His grace. How is that a challenge to you? And how is that a comfort for you?

In what situations or relationships are you quick to compare and judge others as "not good enough" for God's grace? How does 1 Corinthians 4:1-4 speak to what you're doing?

In what situations or relationships are you quick to compare and envy others for what God has given them? How does this parable and John 21 speak to what you're doing?

WRAP-UP: *Session Six*

Jesus' parables have illuminated what the kingdom of God is like, what God Himself is like, and has shown us what it means to obey the first and greatest commandment. We've found God the Father to be generous, impartial in grace, and busily working to cultivate the kingdom.

Jesus' parable about the workers in the vineyard is a perfect segue to Week Seven. The love of God for us and our love for Him always has a communal outworking, for when we're loved, we love our neighbor.

> What's one main takeaway you learned about the King and the kingdom this week?

> How does knowing this truth change the way you relate to God and others?

WATCH THE SESSION SEVEN VIDEO and take notes below. You can find group discussion questions in the leader guide on page 216.

TO ACCESS THE VIDEO TEACHING SESSIONS, USE THE INSTRUCTIONS IN THE BACK OF YOUR BIBLE STUDY BOOK.

165

THE *community* OF THE KINGDOM

SESSION SEVEN

Have you ever met a family that is so collectively passionate about something that when you think of them, you think of what they're passionate about? Perhaps they love mountain biking or camping and are constantly off on adventures together. Perhaps they have a home or farm that's been in their family for generations and their extended family gathers there as much as possible. Perhaps most members of the family have chosen a similar profession, such as a medical career or education. Or maybe they share a mission of bringing outsiders and misfits into their fold.

My family of origin could be characterized by our collective competitiveness. No matter what we're playing or doing, it turns highly (and good-naturedly) competitive. On a different note, thanks to my parents' example, my family values service and jumping in to help where it's needed, whether it's helping a neighbor, volunteering at church, or meeting a need within the family. What about your family? If someone close to you were to name a characteristic about your family of origin, what would they say?

Even more importantly, what is meant to characterize God's family? We are a family, after all. The Bible tells us that the kingdom joins all who put their faith in Christ together as a people.

The invitation of the kingdom is not only to communion with the Father through Christ but also to the fellowship of the saints—to belonging. Our lifelong desire for home and community is ultimately a desire for the kingdom, and this week we'll discover that the church is now, in this life, the living embodiment of the kingdom. God's ongoing cultivation of the kingdom happens by, in, and through the church, with the Spirit fueling and undergirding that work. This kingdom will be fully seen and consummated at Jesus' return, and the church will remain with Him forever.

In the Book of Matthew, Jesus was specific about what kind of community the kingdom forms in and through us and how we're to engage one another within the kingdom. We won't embody the kingdom perfectly in this life, but we reflect the love of the Father and the Son when we love one another in these specific ways. We'll listen to and learn from Jesus as He details the type of love the community of the kingdom is founded and grown upon.

What is meant to characterize the family of God? Let's find out.

Day One

THE KINGDOM IS A FAMILY

God has given us many gifts to enjoy in this life that are meant to be pictures of spiritual truths. Marriage is a picture of the love between Christ and His church. Singleness is a picture of Christ being all-sufficient for us. The Lord's Supper is a visible picture of Christ's body broken for us and His blood poured out on the cross.

Another beautiful gift we're given is adoption. Scripture says we're adopted into the family of God (Eph.1:5). Just as a child is chosen by adoptive parents, brought into the family, and given all the rights as an heir, we too are brought into God's family and given all the riches of Christ.

God's choice to use adoption and family as pictures of who we are has deep implications. Our families are the relationships where we're most intimately known, challenged to grow, and where we mourn and celebrate. They are also the relationships where we're most often hurt but also where we're committed to one another for life.

As we've discovered, the kingdom of God is a *people* who enjoy God's *provision* and rest under His *protective power* in a specific *place*. We're not yet in the place reserved for us in heaven, so presently the kingdom of God is seen in the gathering and relating of the saints—the Church. When we think of the people of God, we should think of the family of God. And we identify ourselves to the world as Christ's disciples by the way we love each other. In our passage today, Jesus uses language that helps us know exactly what type of love this is to be: a familial love. We're to know and be known, challenge one another to grow, mourn, and rejoice together, and work through hurts together.

READ MATTHEW 12:46-50.

1) Skim through Matthew 12 and note what Jesus was doing just prior to this passage.

- 12:15,22:

- 12:24-25,34:

- 12:38:

2) Who were the "people" to whom Jesus spoke (v. 15)?

Jesus asked the man who interrupted His teaching, "Who is my mother, and who are my brothers?" Everyone involved knew the answer, so it seems an odd question to ask. At first, we may read this with a harsh undertone, as if Jesus was excluding or shooing away His biological family. However, if we consider what Jesus was asking as a way of redefining terms, it puts His question in perspective. He wasn't asking about the identities of His biological family; He was asking the man (and the listening crowd) to consider who is included in His spiritual family—the kingdom of God. He expanded the idea of family beyond biological lines, thus indicating an inclusive, generous invitation for anyone who wants to be a part of the kingdom through faith in Him. If they believe, they become a part of the family of God.

Let's dig a bit deeper into this new spiritual family Jesus named.

3) Returning to Matthew 12, what relationships did He say He had within His spiritual family (v. 50)?

4) How had these men and women become His brothers and sisters and mother? (See also Luke 8:21.)

5) What word in verse 49 is used interchangeably with Jesus' spiritual brother, sister, and mother?

6) The use of family language—brother, sister, mother, father—to describe relationships in the church is prominent in the New Testament. First Peter 2:5 says that, for those who are in Christ, we're living stones "being built up as a spiritual house." Read the following passages and note how we're told to relate within the family of God.

PASSAGE	HOW WE'RE TO RELATE WITHIN THE FAMILY
Galatians 6:10	
1 Timothy 5:1-2	
James 2:14-16	
1 John 2:12-14	
1 John 4:21	

7) Because our earthly families consist of sinful people, none of us have experienced ideal familial relationships. But what are family relationships ideally meant to be? What does this indicate the church is meant to be?

The use of familial terms demonstrates that the kingdom of God is highly relational. Jesus' teaching and discipleship happened in relationship as He traveled with His disciples. His rebuke of Peter happened over a meal. He healed through physical presence and touch. He said to John as He hung on the cross, "Here is your mother," and to His mother, "Here is your son" (John 19:26-27, CSB). Through the cross, He brought us into fellowship with the Father and with one another (1 John 1:3).

As the present representation of the kingdom of God, then, the church is intended to be highly relational in all the same ways and highly significant to each of us.

There's something more at play in Matthew 12:46-50 than Jesus redefining familial terms. Jesus' biological family wants His attention. They want Him to stop what He's doing and, in a sense, follow them. But Jesus won't forsake the service of His Father in order to please His earthly family. He demonstrates that biological family doesn't come before God in order of importance and prominence.

> 8) God commands us to love our neighbors, and our spouses, parents, siblings, and children are some of our closest neighbors. How do we reconcile what Jesus did in this passage with what God commands? (See also Matt. 10:37-39.)

Once again, Jesus has opened wide the door of the kingdom, beckoning us into an intimate love of the Father and His Father's family.

Biological family is important, as are our relationships with our spiritual brothers and sisters, but nothing must take the place of our love and devotion to the Father. In fact, we only learn to love well by receiving His love and enjoying fellowship with Him.

Apply

> Do you relate to your local church as a family or in some kind of other way? How would you describe your relationship with others in your church?

> Who are the fathers, mothers, brothers, and sisters in your church that have influenced your faith? Write one of them a letter today, thanking him or her for the way he or she loved and helped you.

> Who is God calling you to be a spiritual parent to? How are you investing in the lives of others?

Day Two

THE KINGDOM IS A FAMILY WHO SERVES ONE ANOTHER

No matter your living situation, you are likely expected to contribute to the household. If you live by yourself, you must take care of everything, from grocery shopping to paying the bills. If you live with roommates, perhaps you've divided up cleaning responsibilities by room. If you're a teenager living with your parents, you may be asked to drive your younger sibling to practices or do the whole household's laundry.

Similarly, the family of God works together to meet the family's needs. Each person has a unique role to play and gifts to help them be a blessing to the whole. But even with our various gifts, as we'll discover in our passage today, Jesus teaches us that we each can make the highest contribution to the household of God: servanthood.

READ MATTHEW 18:1-4.

1) What was the disciples' question of Jesus?

2) Mark 9:33-34 and Luke 9:46 give additional details about what occurred. What was motivating the question?

3) Based upon what we already know about the disciples and what they experienced and participated in, what do you imagine they were evaluating "greatness" based upon?

Though just prior to this discussion Jesus explained that He faced an impending death, the disciples had quickly moved from grief and uncertainty to rivalry. Perhaps they were fighting because Peter, James, and John had been pulled aside for special experiences the others hadn't, such as the Transfiguration. Perhaps they were mulling over Jesus' words in the Sermon on the Mount, in which He made distinctions within the kingdom, saying that some will be "least" and some will be considered "great" (5:19). We don't know specifically, but as Luke wrote, Jesus knew the reasoning of their hearts, and He used it as an opportunity to teach them about true greatness.

In order to answer the question, Jesus pulled a child into their circle and told them they must "turn and become like little children" (18:3). They weren't able to literally become children again, so He had something figurative in mind as He taught.

4) *Turn* is a similar word as *repent*. Of what attitudes and heart-level reasoning did the disciples need to turn from and repent of?

5) Once again, Jesus equated His true disciples with children. What specific mindset did He connect with children in verse 4? How do you frequently see children naturally displaying this mindset?

6) Using a dictionary, write the definition below for *humble* that best fits the context of what Jesus is saying in this passage.

Jesus indicated that humbling oneself is a choice or mindset to take on. While children naturally know their dependence on a parent for care, help, leadership, and direction, we as adults must "turn" back to this dependence, as it doesn't come naturally to us anymore.

7) Putting all of this together, then, how did Jesus define *greatness* in the kingdom? Write out a definition using your own words. (See also Mark 9:35 and Luke 9:48 for help. Read Matt. 23:11-12 for an antonym of *greatness* in the kingdom.)

8) Who were the sons of Zebedee? (See Mark 10:35 for help.)

9) According to Matthew 19:28, what seems to have prompted their mother's request?

10) This mother wanted her sons to have a place of honor similar to Jesus' in the kingdom. Jesus said, "You do not know what you are asking" (20:22), because honor comes through drinking a similar cup to what He would drink. What is this cup to which He's referring? Look at the following references to see what the Bible equates with the cup.

• Isaiah 51:17:

• Revelation 14:9-10:

• When did Jesus drink this cup?

11) James and John would not drink of the cup of God's wrath, but they would, as Jesus said, drink of His cup. What eventually happened to James and John?

• Acts 12:2:

• Revelation 1:9:

• What, then, is the cup to which Jesus referred when talking about what these men faced? How was it different than Jesus' cup?

12) Returning to Matthew 20, how did the other disciples feel when they heard what the mother of James and John had requested? Why might they have felt this way (v. 24)?

13) The disciples wanted to be considered great in the kingdom. Jesus didn't negate that desire and, in fact, He told them how one could be counted as such. Fill in the chart below according to Jesus' explanation in verses 25-28.

	HUMAN IDEA OF GREATNESS	KINGDOM IDEA OF GREATNESS
To what specific examples did Jesus point?		
What characterizes this type of person, according to Jesus?		

14) What repeated word in verse 25 gives us a visual picture of how humans view greatness?

15) Peter gave us a more detailed picture of how someone with authority and influence can use those very God-given leadership opportunities to serve rather than lord over others. Read 1 Peter 5:1-5 and list out what is considered service in the kingdom.

16) Returning to Matthew 20, what reason did Jesus give for why we're to take on a mindset of humility and servanthood (v. 28)? Who, then, is the greatest in the kingdom?

Each of us, as brothers and sisters in the family of God, is identified as a servant. How we serve may vary, but we each are called to serve with the same mindset—that of a dependent, humble child contributing to the household of faith. Our focus is to be like Christ's: not on self but on the good of those around us. This is true greatness in the kingdom, evidenced most beautifully by the King Himself.

Apply

In what areas of your life are you most tempted to seek honor and not humility?

When we sacrificially serve, we're most like our King. How can you cultivate a focus on serving others rather than thinking about who is serving you?

Read Romans 8:16-17 and Philippians 3:10. What "cup" do we drink because we're identified with Christ? How does this give you comfort as you face difficult circumstances?

THE KINGDOM IS A FAMILY
WHO LOVES ONE ANOTHER

As a baby, my youngest son was laid-back and quiet. Aside from when he was hungry, he didn't cry, and even then, his cry wasn't aggressively demanding. If I needed to attend to his older brothers, he'd play contentedly on a blanket. With two other rambunctious boys running around, he was easy to overlook—so easy that, several times, when I was driving the kids around, I panicked at the thought that I might have forgotten to put him in his car seat. His car seat faced backward, so I couldn't peer into the rearview mirror to double-check. Of course, I hadn't forgotten my baby, but I'd ask my two older boys to check, just in case.

Like in any family, there are members of the family of God that we may be prone to overlook or even tempted to look down upon. Jesus addressed this with His disciples in the passage we will consider today.

Jesus continues to reiterate that, in the kingdom of God, His followers are servants who serve and children who are fathered by the perfect Father. Continuing in this theme in today's passage, Jesus will explain that the Father's love for His children is one that we're to emulate with one another. Those who follow Jesus will also highly value all people, especially those who are marginalized by and invisible to the world's esteemed.

READ MATTHEW 18:5-9.

1) Let's recall the scene in which Jesus' teaching took place.

• Who was Jesus teaching (18:1)?

• Where were Jesus and His disciples (17:24)?

• What question sparked this teaching (18:1)?

• What did Jesus choose as a visual teaching tool in order to answer the question (18:2)?

• What did Jesus want His disciples to understand about kingdom community (18:4)?

2) The language Jesus used in verses 5-6 is similar to what He said to His disciples in Matthew 10. Use the verses from Matthew 10 given below to answer the questions.

READ MATTHEW 10:40.

What phrase from this verse is repeated in Matthew 18:5-6?

Was Jesus referring only to literal children in 18:5? Explain your answer.

READ MATTHEW 10:14-15.

What similar concept is used in Matthew 18:5-6?

What response might have caused the disciples to stumble or sin if they weren't careful?

3) What did Jesus mean by "receives" in verse 18:5? How would one receive a child of God in Jesus' name?

The NIV translates verse 6, "If anyone causes one of these little ones—those who believe in me—to stumble ..." Jesus has already explained to the disciples in previous passages that they should expect rejection but to remember that this rejection is ultimately of Christ Himself. Here, He indicated that this rejection, if they weren't on guard against it, could lead them to stumble in their discipleship. It could even lead to serious sin.

4) How might a disciple's rejection by others cause the disciple to stumble in his or her own walk with Jesus? How might it lead to sin?

5) According to Matthew 10:22 and 40, what must the disciple keep in mind in order to stave off stumbling and sin? What additional truth in Matthew 18:6 about God's response to the rejectors was meant to comfort the disciples and keep them from stumbling?

Remember, Jesus had drawn a child into the circle of disciples, an example to them of the humility they were to exhibit. As we humans do, the disciples may have worried what would become of them if they were to stop pursuing their own honor and status and instead become as children—unseen, invisible, and not of important status. Perhaps, too, we can even imagine Jesus pulling the child tenderly into His arms as He spoke these words. As a parent protects his or her child, Jesus explained that God the Father similarly values, sees, and cares for Jesus' disciples. He would exact justice for the disciples who suffered in Jesus' name, and they would be honored by Him within the kingdom.

6) In verses 7-9, Jesus began to speak woe over the world, but He was addressing the disciples. Why do you think He pronounced woe and warned the world about temptation and sin for His disciples to hear?

7) Using a dictionary, write the definition of *woe* that best fits the context of what Jesus was saying.

The language Jesus used in verses 8-9 is similar to what He said to His disciples in Matthew 5.

8) Read Matthew 5:29-30. What similar phrases are used in Matthew 18:8-9? Through the use of hyperbole, what did Jesus indicate He wanted His disciples to do? (Read the verses in the AMP version for help.)

9) If His disciples didn't take their own temptation and sin seriously, what could potentially happen among their brothers and sisters (v. 7)?

10) Paul warned us in Romans 14 about causing our brothers and sisters to stumble regarding issues nonessential to the gospel. According to the following verses, what are some "secondary issues" within the kingdom of God that, if we make primary or essential, can become stumbling blocks to our brothers and sisters?

• Romans 14:1:

• Romans 14:2-3,15,20:

• Romans 14:23:

Not only does God see and honor those who become like children in this world, humbly serving in unseen ways, but Jesus taught that we're to see and honor our brothers and sisters within the family of God. We must not stumble upon our pride of wanting to be seen and esteemed by the world. We also must not cause our brothers and sisters to stumble upon our pride (or any other sin) in a way that causes them to stop following Jesus or miss Jesus entirely. We must humbly love and put others before ourselves, just as God loves us.

Just what does that look like? Jesus told a story to His disciples about how God the Father loves.

READ MATTHEW 18:10-14.

11) Jesus told the disciples they weren't to despise one another as the world despises those they deem of little value. Using a dictionary, write a definition of *despise* below.

12) Jesus implied that there is a specific type of person they should not despise. What describes this person (v. 12)?

13) What reasons did Jesus give for why the disciples shouldn't despise but rather love the one who had gone astray? What would loving one who has gone astray look like if we emulate God?

14) What attributes of God the Father did Jesus detail in today's passage?

Within the kingdom of God, we're brothers and sisters who are loved, sought, and protected by the Father. We're taught by Jesus to emulate this love, specifically considering how our words and actions might lead others to stumble and humbly placing their needs above ours. Not to worry, though. Jesus says our needs are well-known to the Father, and in our humility, we will not be forgotten by Him.

Apply

Is there anything in your life (words, actions, choices) that the Holy Spirit is convicting you is a stumbling block to other believers? Are there preferences that you preach as primary among your brothers and sisters? How would adopting an attitude of humble service impact your life and relationships?

Who is someone in your life that seems to have lost his or her way? How will you purposefully pursue him or her with God's love this week?

Day Four

THE KINGDOM IS A FAMILY WHO FORGIVES ONE ANOTHER

Within the kingdom of God, we're a family: fathers, mothers, brothers, and sisters. Each of us are called to serve, love, and care for one another as Christ has loved us. However, just as at some point in our biological families we hurt or offend our siblings, we inevitably will wound or be wounded by our spiritual brothers and sisters.

In our passage today, Jesus teaches His disciples what to do when sin affects relationships within kingdom community. Just as He did in yesterday's passage, He gives the disciples instruction on how to navigate broken relationships and then offers a story to illustrate His point. We have much to learn and apply, so let's jump right in.

READ MATTHEW 18:15-20.

1) What occurrence within kingdom community was Jesus preemptively addressing (v. 15)?

2) What did Jesus teach His disciples to do first if a brother or sister sins against them (v. 15)?

3) Jesus emphasized the private nature of approaching a brother or sister who has sinned against us. Scripture has more to say about how this private encounter should be handled.

• According to Galatians 6:1, with what demeanor should we approach our brothers and sisters?

• According to Ephesians 4:15, with what motivation should we approach them?

How are we to relate to the one who has sinned?

• Proverbs 27:6:

• 2 Thessalonians 3:14-15:

4) Returning to Matthew 18, what did Jesus mean by "listens"? How would one know if the person has "listened"? What is the outcome when the person has listened?

5) Fill in the chart with the process Jesus gave us for approaching someone who has sinned against us and *doesn't* listen to our private plea.

WHAT TO DO WHEN THE PRIVATE PLEA GOES UNHEEDED
Next Step:
Does Not Listen
Next Step:
Does Not Listen
Next Step:

6) The confrontation of sin moves from private to more of a public or formal charge. How do we obey this instruction of bringing two or three witnesses without also falling into the sin of gossip or maligning a reputation?

7) What is the goal of confronting a brother or sister who is in habitual sin (v. 15, see also 1 Cor. 5:4-5)?

8) Jesus tells us to go to those who have sinned against us for the purpose of restoring right relationship to God and to one another. We must be careful not to confuse personal preference, conviction on secondary issues, or annoyance with sin. What kinds of behaviors and actions might Jesus be thinking of here? (See Rom.16:17-18; 1 Cor. 5:9-13; Gal. 5:19-21.)

Jesus then repeated to the disciples what He had previously told Peter: "Whatever you bind on earth shall be bound in heaven, and whatever you loose on earth shall be loosed in heaven" (Matt. 18:18). Jesus extended the authority He'd previously given Peter alone to all the apostles, the future leaders of the church. He gave them authority to proclaim the kingdom, as well as to proclaim what is true and false, right and wrong.

Peter stepped forward to ask a question, possibly considering this authority Jesus shared with him and drawing off the theme of forgiveness. Jesus told a story in response.

READ MATTHEW 18:21-22.

Jews taught and practiced that one should forgive three times (Job 33:29-30; Amos 1:3), so Peter's suggestion of forgiving seven times goes far beyond what he believes is expected. Jesus answered with "seventy-seven times." It's not that His disciples should keep count, forgiving right up to seventy-seven times and then no more. For the disciple of Jesus, forgiveness should characterize his or her life. Jesus told a parable to illustrate what He meant.

READ MATTHEW 18:23-35.

9) To what did Jesus liken the kingdom of heaven (v. 23)?

10) According to verse 24, what did the first servant owe?

A talent equals about twenty years of wages. In today's terms, one talent = about six hundred thousand dollars, so ten thousand talents would be roughly six billion dollars.[25]

11) The first servant said to his master, "I will pay you everything." Was it actually possible for the servant to pay back his debt?

12) What two things did the master do for the first servant (v. 27)?

13) Fill in the chart below according to what Jesus communicated in the parable.

Who did the master represent?	
Who did the first servant represent?	
What did the debt represent?	
Who did the fellow servants represent?	

14) The second servant owed the first servant one hundred denarii, which is about twenty weeks' wages. In today's terms, that's roughly twelve thousand dollars. Was this a significant debt? What do you think Jesus was conveying about the relationship and debt between the servants?

15) After what the first servant had just experienced, wouldn't we expect him to forgive the second servant's debt? What did he do instead?

16) What does the distress of the watching fellow servants (v. 31) teach us about the consequences of unforgiveness within kingdom community?

Jesus indicated through the parable that a person who truly understands the grace and mercy they've been shown by God will also be merciful and forgiving toward his or her brothers and sisters when sinned against. Who are we to hold a small debt over a brother or sister's head when God has forgiven all our sins in Christ?

Forgiveness is not saying, "It doesn't matter," or "It's OK. Let's move on," or "The past is the past. Just forget about it." Forgiveness doesn't attempt to ignore a wound as if it didn't happen. Biblical forgiveness means there is a debt to be paid—a wrong has been done and that wrong has had consequences—but we're choosing to erase the person's debt to us. We don't expect them to somehow make up for what's been done. Forgiveness isn't typically instantaneous, but rather a continued choice not to renew or count up someone's debt again. We can only do this by recognizing and resting in the all-encompassing mercy we've been shown through Jesus. The kingdom family is one characterized by this kind of repentance and forgiveness.

Apply

Is there someone who has sinned against you within the family of God with whom you need to talk? Ask God to help you know whether or not to go to the person and talk with him or her about it. Ask God for the demeanor of gentleness, the motivation of love, and the goal of restoring fellowship.

Considering the parable of the unforgiving servant, from whom are you withholding mercy? How does considering the insurmountable debt you've been forgiven of help you see that person in a new way?

THE KINGDOM IS A FAMILY
WHO INVITES OUTSIDERS IN

Many people I know who became Christians when they were teenagers did so because a friend's family loved them, invited them into their home, fed them, showed interest in them, listened to their worries, and eventually shared the gospel with them. One such person told me that it was specifically the love she saw between family members that drew her in and made her wonder what set this family apart as different than her own. The mother listened to her children and made the home a safe place for them to learn from their mistakes. The man of the house treated his wife with tenderness and respect. What, she wondered, caused them to act this way?

So far this week, we've learned that the kingdom of God is a spiritual family, characterized by service, forgiveness, and love. This love, the apostle John records Jesus as saying, is how those outside the family recognize we're His disciples: "Love one another: just as I have loved you, you also are to love one another. By this all people will know that you are my disciples, if you have love for one another" (John 13:34-45).

The community of the kingdom itself is an invitation to outsiders. But as Jesus makes clear in our passage for today, we're not to wait for others to discover this community for themselves. We're to actively seek outsiders and invite them, through our love and our own discipleship, into the community of the kingdom.

1) READ MATTHEW 28:16-20. LET'S FIRST SET THE SCENE FOR JESUS' FINAL WORDS TO THE DISCIPLES.

What has just taken place (28:1-6)?

Why were there only eleven disciples with Jesus after His resurrection (27:3-5)?

Why were they in Galilee (28:7)?

What is significant about Jesus, the disciples, and Galilee (4:18,23,25)?

This passage—the end of Jesus' ministry on earth—bookends the beginning of His ministry. The disciples were called to follow Jesus in Galilee, and now they've gathered again in Galilee, having seen Him conquer sin and death through His death and resurrection. The church will soon be born, built upon Christ as the head and empowered by the Holy Spirit. When the disciples see Him, they worship, while some in the larger group of disciples doubt Him. What will Jesus say in His parting words to all those gathered on the mountain?

2) What did Jesus reveal about Himself in verse 18? Why do you think He led with this statement?

3) What does Jesus have authority over, as confirmed by His resurrection? Fill in the chart according to the following Scriptures:

VERSE(S)	WHAT JESUS HAS AUTHORITY OVER
John 17:1-2	
Ephesians 1:20-22	
Colossians 2:10	
1 Peter 3:22	

4) On Week One, Day Four, Questions 1, 2, and 3, what else did you record Jesus as having authority over?

5) Who has given Jesus this authority? (See Matt. 11:27.)

6) As He promised He'd do, Jesus shared His authority with the disciples. Returning to Matthew 28, what is the command Jesus gave them regarding how they're to use their gifted authority?

7) What two components will making disciples entail?

8) What does baptism represent?

All along Jesus has been preparing the disciples for this moment. Perhaps as they listened to His final words and anticipated their friend's imminent departure, they mentally scrolled through the memories of what they'd seen, heard, and done alongside Jesus. He'd called them from their fishing nets, saying, "Follow me, and I will make you fishers of men" (Matt. 4:19). They'd marveled as He calmed storms and turned water into wine. He'd taught them the message and culture of the kingdom of God, and He'd modeled for them how to live according to this kingdom. He'd then sent them out, two-by-two, to preach this kingdom, and they'd returned with both excitement and questions.

Now it is their turn to continue the ministry that Jesus began. They are now the proclaimers of the kingdom. They are the ones who will administer mercy and justice. They are the ones who will exhibit grace and truth, just as Jesus did. They are no longer just disciples but also disciple-makers, and their love for one another will lead the way.

Jesus did, the disciples observed. Jesus did, the disciples helped. The disciples did, Jesus helped them. The disciples were to go and do, while others observed.

From that moment on the mountain, the pattern of disciple-making will continue for generations, for we in this current day know the gospel of the kingdom because of Jesus and these men. They were faithful to do what Jesus commissioned them to do in His last hour with them.

As recorded in the Book of Acts, Peter preached to the masses and the church was born. He, John, and Matthew wrote books, canonized in the New Testament, in order to train and equip the church. Paul, Barnabas, and James (the brother of Jesus) joined the list of the apostles. Most of the apostles died a painful death, a persecution Jesus predicted. But the gospel of the kingdom went forth, and we're the beneficiaries. The mission hasn't changed. As disciples of Jesus, we too are called to be disciple-makers. We're to involve ourselves in passing our faith in Christ to the next generation like a link in a continuous chain. We're to spiritually reproduce, extending and inviting others into the kingdom family.

9) Thinking back to what we've learned about Jesus' ministry, if we were to emulate the way Jesus helped His disciples internalize the kingdom message, what would be priorities in our relationships with others?

10) Record insights from the following passages about what disciple-making entails.

VERSE(S)	WHAT DISCIPLE-MAKING ENTAILS
Colossians 1:28-29	
1 Thessalonians 2:8	
2 Timothy 2:2	
Titus 2:3-8	

11) What promise are we to remember to undergird our mission as disciple-makers (Matt. 28:20b)?

Apply

In his book, *Transforming Discipleship,* Greg Ogden provides a helpful framework for discipleship that encapsulates these Scriptures:

> Discipleship is an intentional relationship in which we walk alongside other disciples in order to encourage, equip, and challenge one another in love to grow toward maturity in Christ through the authority and power of God's Word.[26]

Who in your life are you intentionally pursuing to share the gospel with? If no one, who has God brought to mind as you've studied today's lesson as someone He wants you to pursue and share with?

Who in your life are you intentionally passing your faith onto? If no one, who in your life needs help growing toward maturity in Christ? Write their names in the margin. Pray about asking them to study Scripture with you, apply it to your lives, and pray together on a regular basis.[27]

WRAP-UP: *Session Seven*

Kingdom community as Jesus describes it is fueled by love, forgiveness, mercy, and service. It is also hospitable toward outsiders: a display of love between disciples is a warm invitation for the lost to come to Christ and His church. Once again, the cultivation of kingdom community requires each disciple's dependence upon the Holy Spirit to enable us to do what doesn't come naturally to us in our flesh.

What's one main takeaway you learned about the King and the kingdom this week?

How does knowing this truth change the way you relate to God and others?

WATCH THE SESSION EIGHT VIDEO and take notes below. You can find group discussion questions in the leader guide on page 216.

TO ACCESS THE VIDEO TEACHING SESSIONS, USE THE INSTRUCTIONS IN THE BACK OF YOUR BIBLE STUDY BOOK.

191

THE *kingdom* TO COME

SESSION EIGHT

The first time I encountered true suffering—one that I knew would never really go away—was when my husband and I were given a difficult diagnosis for our three-year-old son. My whole world turned upside down, and I fell into a deep grief and, eventually, a profound rethinking of my worldview. At the core of this rethinking was, "Is God really good? How can I reconcile a good God that Scripture says does all things well with the reality of what I'm facing?"

I realized over time that my worldview had very much been that if I obey God, He will give me what I consider good, which meant nothing negative or difficult. I also realized that my hopes had been in temporary things or in my own carefully constructed agenda for my life. I would have said my hope was in God, sure, but it was also very much in the here and now.

Scripture often connects trials and suffering with truths about eternity. I didn't know much about eternity, nor what awaited me in heaven, so I started reading, learning, and studying as much as I could get my hands on. I began to realize Scripture connects suffering to truths about heaven, because when we know what awaits us, we can better endure the trials of life. We can better distinguish what's temporary from what's eternal, and our true hope begins to solidify.

There is, as you may already have noted, an "already, not yet" nature to the kingdom of God. Jesus announced the kingdom had come, because He had come, and through His death and resurrection He established His good and gracious reign over this kingdom. His work on the cross was essentially His crowning ceremony, the moment He claimed authority over all things, including death.

Currently, we benefit from His finished work, but we wait for the day when the mysterious, unseen kingdom is made visible and all bow before King Jesus. An understanding that we're in an "already, not yet" time is vital, because when we get this confused, thinking all is finished now, we easily get disoriented and even led astray by our own misconceptions about God or unfulfilled expectations of what we think He should be doing in this time.

Instead, we remember that the kingdom is presently built in and through God's church and that the kingdom is also yet to come in its fullness. Our hope grows upon the promise that one day it will be fully realized, when pain and tears will be no more.

In our final week together, we will study the coming kingdom, as described by Jesus in what is often referred to as His Olivet Discourse before He went to the cross. And in light of what is to come in the future, we'll answer the question, "How then do we now live?"

THE COMING KINGDOM'S BIRTH PAINS

Every birth is preceded by various signs of the baby's impending arrival: the mother's cervix dilates, the womb contracts, and her water breaks. However, the strongest indication that the awaited time has drawn near is pain. Every labor is marked by struggle and pain as a mother gives birth to a new life.

As Jesus neared the end of His time on earth, He told of many things to come—all of them laborious birth pains as the world will give way to the life and joy of the new heavens and the new earth. This time, He said, would be marked by struggle, confusion, and darkness, but He foretold these events so His disciples would be prepared and would endure until the very end.

We're those disciples, and we must not only prepare ourselves but also live in light of what Jesus says is to come.

READ MATTHEW 24:3-14.

1) Matthew set the scene for us in verse 3. Record the details he gave below.

• Where did this scene take place?

• From what we've learned previously, what is the significance of Jesus being seated as He taught?

• Who was on the scene?

• What were the disciples and Jesus discussing that prompted Jesus' teaching? (See also vv. 1-2.)

2) What specific question did the disciples ask Jesus at the end of verse 3?

3) To what "coming" and "end of age" were they referring?
(See Matt. 13:39 and 24:27.)

4) In verses 4-8, Jesus detailed initial signs to look for in order to know the end of the age is near and the kingdom is coming. In the box below, list the signs Jesus named.

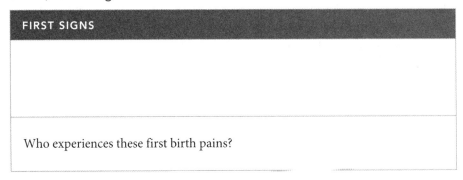

FIRST SIGNS

Who experiences these first birth pains?

5) What instructions or warnings did Jesus give His disciples regarding these first signs?

Jesus said that as the birth pains began in the world, they would be painful enough to cause alarm among His disciples. However, the end is not yet; more signs will come and, as labor contractions do, they will increase in severity.

6) In verses 9-14, Jesus described additional signs of the kingdom coming. In the box below, list the second wave of signs Jesus named.

SECOND SIGNS

Who experiences these second set of birth pains?

7) What instruction or warning did Jesus imply regarding these second signs?

The second set of signs will cut to the core of the church, dividing brothers and sisters. Those disciples who remain will experience the heartbreak of some falling away from the faith. The disciples are called to endure in both their first love—remaining devoted to Christ—and in fulfilling their mission.

8) According to verse 14, what will happen in the final days before the earthly kingdom passes away and the new kingdom comes?

NOW READ MATTHEW 24:15-28.

9) In verses 15-28, Jesus continued predicting birth pains, and they are very severe in nature. List what will happen in this third wave of signs.

THIRD SIGNS
Who experiences this third set of birth pains?

10) We don't know exactly what the "abomination of desolation" (v. 15) is that Daniel spoke about, but Paul gave us a further clue in 2 Thessalonians 2:3-4. According to these verses, what should Jesus' disciples look for at this abomination?

11) What instruction or warning did Jesus give regarding this third set of signs?

12) Much like Pharaoh's sorcerers tried to match the miraculous acts of Moses and Aaron in Exodus, Jesus said there will be false prophets who perform signs and wonders that will cause His disciples to wonder if the false prophets are, in fact, the Christ. How can we discern whether or not someone is a false prophet, according to 1 John 2:22-23?

13) What act of mercy will God show to His people during this great tribulation, according to verse 22?

14) Jesus seemed to indicate that much of the confusion during these final birth pangs will center around whether or not Christ has returned. Check below which best describes what the return of Christ will be like based upon verse 27.

☐ Public and clear to all

☐ Secret and dependent on us or another person to discover

15) Finally, after great labor, the birth of the kingdom will be at hand. According to Jesus, what will be the final signs before the kingdom comes?

FINAL SIGNS
Who will experience the final signs?

16) Why will the tribes of the earth mourn when they see Jesus returning? (See Rev. 1:7; 19:11-16.)

And then! Jesus will gather His disciples to Himself and bring us with Him into the kingdom of God. We will rest under His rule and reign forever, and a new heavens and a new earth will be born after a long and difficult labor. Whether or not we're in the specific stages Jesus talked about in Matthew 24, we definitely feel the labor pains of living in this world. Giving our imagination to the kingdom to come, one day birthed from these pains, brings joy, peace, and longing and helps us endure to the end.

Apply

READ ROMANS 8:22-27.

What's currently causing you to groan with longing for the future kingdom?

What specifically helps you hope and wait with patience?

What does it mean to you that the Spirit is interceding for you according to God's will? What does this teach you about the nature of God and your relationship with Him?

THE COMING KINGDOM'S ARRIVAL

Long before labor starts, a birth is preceded by preparation. Parents circle the due date on the calendar and get to work. They put the crib together, register for gifts, and paint the nursery. They attend childbirth classes and read about what they can expect. They go to doctor's appointments to make sure both mother and child are healthy. For nine months, their lives revolve around that circled due date.

In yesterday's study, we read descriptions of the birth pains Jesus predicted will precede His second coming. He answered the disciples' second recorded question: "What will be the sign of your coming and of the end of the age?" In today's passage, Jesus continued what is often called His Olivet Discourse, detailing the *timing* of these future events in answer to the disciples' first question: "When will these things be?"

READ MATTHEW 24:32-33.

1) Let's recall the scene Matthew has set for us in verse 3.

• Where did this scene take place?

• Who was on the scene?

2) In the previous passage, Jesus compared the signs of His impending arrival to birth pains. Here, He compared the signs to agriculture and seasonal changes. What does the budding leaf on the fig tree tell is coming (v. 32)?

3) What do you do, think of, or prepare for when summer is on the near horizon? How is this time of year different for you than other seasons?

4) In regard to the fig tree leaves, Jesus said, "So also, when you see all these things, you know that he is near, at the very gates." As we consider the preparations we make as spring turns to summer, what was Jesus communicating to His disciples?

READ MATTHEW 24:34-44.

In verse 34, Jesus pivoted from addressing specific signs to addressing the time when the kingdom will come. He said a curious thing: "Truly, I say to you, this generation will not pass away until all these things take place."

5) Who is "this generation" and what are "these things"? (Scholars debate the answer but recall verses 3-28 for a possibility.)

• This generation =

• These things =

6) Fill in the chart according to verse 35 and by looking up the following verses: Psalm 102:25-26; Isaiah 51:6; 1 Corinthians 13:8-12; Hebrews 12:26-29; 2 Peter 3:10; and Revelation 21:1-4.

WHAT WILL PASS AWAY WHEN JESUS COMES AGAIN?	WHAT WILL LAST OR BEGIN WHEN JESUS COMES AGAIN?

7) Who knows the timing of Jesus' return and the kingdom's arrival (v. 36)?

Verse 37 says, "For as were the days of Noah, so will be the coming of the Son of Man." Jesus used similar language in verse 27: "For as the lightning comes from the east and shines as far as the west, so will be the coming of the Son of Man." Both indicate a sudden onset of rain after specific signs of warning.

8) How did Jesus describe the days of Noah in verses 38-39? How does Genesis 6:11-12 add to your understanding of what characterized the days of Noah?

9) In verse 39, what primary word did Jesus use to describe the people living in the days of Noah? Using an online thesaurus, what synonym for this adjective best fits Jesus' use of this word?

10) In response to all He's told them, Jesus commanded His disciples to "stay awake" (v. 42). What did He mean by this figurative choice of words?

READ 1 THESSALONIANS 5:1-8.

11) What word pictures did Paul use that are similar to Jesus' words in Matthew 24?

12) Verse 3 gives an additional description of the "unaware" people. What was their refrain, and what did they mean by it?

13) Paul gave specific descriptions and instructions of what it means to "stay awake" in verse 8. List them in the chart below.

STAY AWAKE

Both Jesus and the apostle Paul want us to be watchful, alert, and awake to the things of God and His coming kingdom. We must not become spiritually apathetic, dull, nor filled by the things of the world that mute our sensitivity to the Holy Spirit. Why? Because we do not know the hour of the coming of the Son of Man, and if ever we were ready for anything, we will want to be in Christ, ready to see the face of our Beloved.

Apply

Looking back at the chart on Question 6, would you say you're spending your mental energy, time, and affections on what will pass away or what will last?

Are there areas of your life where you've become spiritually deadened or apathetic? What contributes to that state that needs to change?

What are ways we as Christians can be watchful now? What might that look like in modern life?

Day Three

THE COMING KINGDOM IS DELAYED

My oldest son, at seventeen, traveled alone for the first time on an airplane from Texas to Virginia. My parents saw him safely through security, and I picked him up when he got off the plane, but the middle part of his trip was what I worried most about—he had to change planes. When his first plane landed, he texted me when he got to his gate, and I breathed a sigh of relief. But then the airline notices started popping up on my phone. His flight was delayed. And then delayed again. In all, the flight was delayed five times. Afternoon was turning into early evening, and I had no idea what I'd do if he got stuck in North Carolina by himself. I kept refreshing the flight details on the airline's app; the delay was all I could think about. Finally, my son texted: "I'm on the plane, and we're about to take off." Relief flooded over me.

Delays aren't easy to navigate. For Christians, the delay of Christ's return is the most difficult of all. Because the kingdom is coming, Jesus says we must be awake, watching and waiting. In today's study, Jesus tells two parables in order to illustrate His point and to give further instructions to His listening disciples. The first parable tells the story of two servants. Jesus uses this parable to teach His disciples what they are to do as they watch and wait.

READ MATTHEW 24:45-51.

1) Based upon parables we've studied in previous weeks, identify the characters in the story Jesus told. (See Week Six, Day Four for help.)

• Who did the servant represent?

• Who did the master represent?

• What is a steward?

2) Fill in the chart below according to the parable Jesus told.

	SERVANT #1	SERVANT #2
What descriptors did Jesus use for this servant?	(vv. 45-46)	(vv. 48,51)
What did this servant do in his role?		
What was the outcome for this servant?		

3) What did Jesus mean when He said His faithful disciples would be set over all that He possessed? (See 2 Tim. 2:11-13.)

In this parable, one is a believing servant—a true disciple—and the other is a disbelieving servant—a false disciple. The unbelieving servant says to himself, "My master is delayed," which indicates he knows his rightful place. But he has rejected the master's role, believing the master won't return after all. The unbelieving servant seems to say, *I will not have to answer to him. I can and will do as I please. My soul and actions will never be accounted for.* His actions hurt his fellow servants and, as the people in the days of Noah, he "slumbers" in his drunkenness. His desire is for his own will to be done.

Believing servants may at times also wonder where the master is and when he's going to return, just as David cried out, "How long, O LORD?" (Ps. 13:1) and the martyrs cry for the Lord to judge and avenge injustice (Rev. 6:10). Their question about God's delay, however, is filled with trust and longing, and a desire for His will to finally and completely be done.

4) What does this parable tell us about what we're to do as Jesus' disciples while waiting for the kingdom to come? In other words, what do we want Him to find us doing upon His return?

Continuing in the theme of watching and waiting, Jesus now begins a second parable about ten bridesmaids.

READ MATTHEW 25:1-13.

In biblical times, a betrothal period—typically around a year—occurred after a man and woman were engaged. The man would return to his father's home in order to build an addition onto the home for him and his new bride. When the home addition was complete and the father of the groom gave his blessing, the groom would return to marry his bride. The bride, meanwhile, prepared herself and her garments for the marriage ceremony, keeping herself pure for her groom and keeping her lamps trimmed and ready, in case the groom came at night. Finally, the wedding would begin with the groom and his groomsmen parading together with great joy through the streets of the city to the bride's home. The bride would hear the groom and his wedding party approaching and go out to meet him, and her bridesmaids too. After the wedding, the entire party would proceed back to the father of the groom's house for a wedding feast.

5) Identify the characters in the parable.

- Who does the bridegroom represent?

- Who do the bridesmaids represent?

- What does the wedding feast represent? (See Rev. 19:7-10.)

6) The bridesmaids who aren't prepared and miss entry to the wedding feast are told, "Truly, I say to you, I do not know you" (v. 12). Read this verse in the Amplified version of the Bible. In what way are these women not prepared?

7) Notably, in this parable, the groom is delayed. What is one reason God delays the return of Jesus, according to 2 Peter 3:9?

8) What command does Jesus want His disciples to obey (v. 13)?

9) Using a dictionary, write a definition for *watch* below that best fits the context of Jesus' parable. Give an example of how a Christian practices watchfulness.

Many of Jesus' parables end with a division of people: one group is brought into the kingdom and one group of people is sent away to a place where there is weeping and gnashing of teeth. Such a clear distinction is often rightly sobering and may at times even strike fear in our hearts. For the unbeliever—the one who lives for self and believes no master will ever hold him or her accountable—this fear is good, for it's made to make one consider the state of his or her soul. We have the opportunity now to "wake up," repent of our sins, and believe in Jesus for the salvation of our souls.

For the Christian, however, these stories, while certainly an opportunity to allow God to test our hearts for saving faith, are primarily meant to be comforting. The King may be delayed and suffering may be long, but He is coming for His bride. We will go with Him into the marriage feast and live with Him forever.

Apply

In what ways does the delay of the coming kingdom cause you to doubt God and live for yourself? How can you cultivate a watchfulness instead?

Jesus said that when He comes again, His true disciples will be found faithful in fulfilling the mission of making disciples. How does this give you perspective on your purpose in this life?

In Hebrews 10:25, the writer says, "[Encourage] one another, and all the more as you see the Day drawing near." In other words, we're to encourage one another with the truth that our King and Bridegroom is returning for us. Who in your life needs this encouragement today? How will you give them that encouragement?

Day Four

THE COMING KINGDOM
BEGINS WITH JUDGMENT

We've seen that Jesus has communicated with His disciples about the signs preceding the coming of the kingdom and how we're to live as He is delayed in coming. We pick up today as Jesus' discourse continues, describing the actual coming of the kingdom and how this coming will begin. It begins with a sorting, a judgment, and a reward for those who are in Christ.

1) Read Matthew 25:31-46. In what way will Jesus come that will be seen by all people (v. 31)? How does Revelation 19:11-16 add to your understanding of the manner in which He will come?

2) Who will come with Him (v. 31)?

3) The throne in verse 31 illustrates Jesus' kingship and dominion, but it also represents judgment. Using a dictionary, write a definition below of *judgment* that fits the context of what Jesus will do on His throne.

4) What do the following passages teach us about Jesus' seat of judgment?

• Romans 14:10-12:

• 2 Corinthians 5:10:

• Revelation 20:11-15:

5) Who will stand before Jesus as He sits on His throne of authority and judgment (v. 32)?

6) What will be Jesus' first act as Judge (v. 32)?

7) Who do the sheep represent, and who do the goats represent? Below, next to each animal, write the descriptors Scripture uses for sheep and goats.

- Sheep (v. 37):
- Goats (Matt. 13:49):

8) Fill in the chart below according to the actions Jesus describes each "animal" doing in Matthew 25:31-46.

SHEEP	GOATS

9) Is it the actions and behaviors of the sheep that gained them entry into the kingdom? Is it the lack of action that kept the goats out? In other words, how is someone deemed righteous or unrighteousness?

Judgment often carries a negative connotation and, even for the Christian, can appear frightening. We're often afraid because we've seen unjust judgments made by fellow humans or injustices go unchecked. We're also often afraid of judgment before God because we know the darkness and struggle of our own heart, or we may have an unbiblical idea of who God is. We must, then, have a right understanding of this final judgment and of the Judge sitting on the throne.

Jesus doesn't judge as humans do. We rarely have all the information or understand all the angles, but Jesus is the perfect Judge and does all things right. He knows all things and how to pronounce perfect judgment. He won't be unjust with us or with anyone else. In addition, Jesus' throne is called a "throne of grace" (Heb. 4:16). He willingly gives grace and mercy to anyone who has come asking for it. In fact, the standard by which the judgment will take place as described in Matthew 25 is Jesus Himself. If we've come under the blood of Jesus by faith for the forgiveness and cleansing of our sins, we've been declared righteous in the sight of God. We've been granted mercy, which will be declared at the judgment seat as we're sorted off as sheep. Our faith will have proven itself in good works, as described by Jesus as hospitality, meeting needs, and visiting the prisoner. In other words, what the "sheep" do is evidence of their faith.

For those who have resisted or rejected Jesus, they have only their deeds to bring before the judgment seat. Even one unrighteous deed makes us fully unrighteous, and with only unrighteousness to bring, one is not covered by the blood of Jesus and will therefore incur the just wrath of God. These will be sorted as goats.

10) What is the reward for the righteous (vv. 34,46)?

11) What is the outcome for the unrighteous (v. 46)?

12) Verse 34 says the righteous will inherit the kingdom of God. How does Scripture describe this coming kingdom? Fill in the chart below according to the passages given.

VERSE(S)	WHAT IS THE FUTURE KINGDOM LIKE?
2 Timothy 4:8	
1 Peter 1:3-4	
Revelation 7:9-10	
Revelation 21:1-5	
Revelation 21:22-27	
Revelation 22:1-5	

What a beautiful picture of the inheritance of the saints! As Scripture's final words say, "Come, Lord Jesus!" (Rev. 22:20).

Apply

Does the idea of the judgment seat fill you with longing or with dread? Explain your answer.

What from the passages you read on Question 11 are you most looking forward to about the future kingdom?

Day Five
THE COMING KINGDOM CONTINUALLY REMEMBERED

My friend, Valeri, married Craig, a JAG lawyer, a few months before he deployed to Afghanistan for twelve months. Valeri didn't know the exact time or date he'd come back, even up to the last hour before his return, but she told me she thought about his return every day. She even started preparing for his return as soon as he left: they set goals to pay off debt and made plans for a celebratory trip. She committed to exercising and bought a new dress she planned to wear when he returned. As the approximate date drew near, she booked a photographer for the reunion photos and purchased his favorite foods. Even if he returned in the middle of the night, there was no way she was going to miss welcoming him home.

The biblical word that describes Valeri is *watchful*. She was alert, ready, prepared for action, and wouldn't let herself be caught unaware.

What would it look like for us to be watchful? To keep awake and sober as we wait for Jesus to return? The images Jesus uses of a mother giving birth or a bride waiting for her groom give us a picture of intimate love. Each of these show that being watchful is not about making sure we don't get caught with our hand in the cookie jar or making sure the good scale outweighs the bad scale at the particular moment Jesus returns. Being watchful is about longing. We're to consider how we can stir up our longing for Christ and our life with Him forever.

We come to the end of our study today, and we'll end in what may at first seem an unusual passage. This week, we've focused on the coming kingdom, discovering signs preceding the King's arrival, ways we're to be prepared for the kingdom's arrival, and what the coming kingdom will be like. But we remain in this present day, this in-between space, waiting, watching, and longing. Jesus gave His disciples instructions on what to do in this present day, some of which we've already studied in previous weeks. However, He gives His disciples a *specific* way of waiting, watching, and longing—an act of remembrance and proclamation until He returns.

READ MATTHEW 26:26-29.

1) What meal were Jesus and His disciples eating? (See Matt. 26:17.)

2) What event did the Passover meal mark in the life of the nation of Israel, and why were they to observe it each year? (See Ex. 12:24-27.)

3) What specifically caused God to pass over or spare the firstborn sons in the families of Israel? (See Ex. 12:3,7,12-13.)

4) As they ate the Passover meal, Jesus identified Himself as the very components of the meal. How do the components symbolize Him?

• A lamb without blemish, slaughtered:

• Unleavened bread (Hint: in the Bible, leaven represents sin):

• Wine:

5) Why did Jesus tell His disciples to ingest His body and blood? (See John 6:53-54.)

After God instituted the Passover, as recorded in Exodus, He also called the Israelites to consecrate their firstborn sons, saying,

You shall set apart to the LORD all that first opens the womb.
All the firstborn of your animals that are males shall be the LORD's.
Every firstborn of a donkey you shall redeem with a lamb, or if you will
not redeem it you shall break its neck. Every firstborn of man among
your sons you shall redeem. And when in time to come your son asks
you, "What does this mean?" you shall say to him, "By a strong hand
the LORD brought us out of Egypt, from the house of slavery. For when
Pharaoh stubbornly refused to let us go, the LORD killed all the firstborn
in the land of Egypt, both the firstborn of man and the firstborn
of animals. Therefore I sacrifice to the LORD all the males that first
open the womb, but all the firstborn of my sons I redeem."
EXODUS 13:12-15

6) Does Jesus fulfill this observance or turn it on its head? Explain your thinking.

At Passover, there are traditionally four cups of wine, each representing a promise God made in Exodus 6:6-7: *I will bring you out, I will deliver, I will redeem,* and *I will take.* The cup Jesus drank with His disciples is likely the third: *I will redeem.* The exact wording in Exodus 6:6 is, "I will redeem you with an outstretched arm and with great acts of judgment." By telling His disciples to eat of His body and drink of His blood, soon spilled out, He was referencing an absorption of God's wrath on their behalf and in its place offering the forgiveness of sins—redemption.

7) We still observe this meal in the church today—what we often call the Lord's Supper. Why, as non-Jews, do we observe this meal? Read 1 Corinthians 11:23-26 and write the two reasons below.

• 11:24-25:

• 11:26:

As we wait for the coming kingdom, we remember and proclaim that Jesus our King gave His life so that we might have it eternally. To remember and proclaim is the work of the gathered church, where we see and experience the kingdom of God in our present day. To remember and proclaim keeps our faith a flame, burning with longing for the coming kingdom.

8) Who is also waiting with us for the kingdom to come (Matt. 26:29)?

What is our prayer as we wait, remembering and proclaiming Jesus the King? It is, of course, the prayer Jesus taught His disciples: "Our Father in heaven, hallowed be your name. Your kingdom come, your will be done, on earth as it is in heaven" (Matt. 6:9-10).

We remember. We wait. We watch, expectantly, for our coming King.

Apply

How do you remember the redemption Jesus bought you? How do you keep it at the forefront of your heart and mind?

What are the things in your daily life that stir your desires for God's kingdom? What things take away those desires?

Why is it important to meet with the gathered church as we wait for the coming kingdom?

WRAP-UP: *Session Eight*

In His Olivet Discourse, which we studied this week, Jesus described the signs His disciples should look for at the end of the age—the signs that His return is imminent and the kingdom of God will be fully realized. The return of Jesus is characterized by a groom coming for his bride: the exact time is unknown, so the bride must be alert and prepared, waiting expectantly for the joy of the groom's voice in the streets. And so, we wait. We watch. And we place our hope in the coming Christ.

What's one main takeaway you learned about the King and the kingdom this week?

How does knowing this truth change the way you relate to God and others?

TO ACCESS THE VIDEO TEACHING SESSIONS, USE THE INSTRUCTIONS IN THE BACK OF YOUR BIBLE STUDY BOOK.

CONCLUSION

By now, I hope the definition of the kingdom of God has imprinted on your heart and mind: the kingdom of God is a *people* who enjoy God's *provision* and rest under His *protective power* in a specific *place*. Even more, I pray your affection for and awe of King Jesus has grown. He has come for us! And because of His service to God through His perfectly lived life, His death on the cross, and His resurrection from the grave, He rules and reigns over this kingdom.

Because we've followed after King Jesus, confessing our sin and accepting by faith His work on our behalf, we've come under His benevolent reign. We come under His perfect *provision*—for our sins and for our everyday lives—and His *power*. Everything the King has, He shares with us.

We're brought together into the kingdom as a *people*, the family of God. We're to be known by our love and service, our forgiveness and humility. The kingdom is characterized by blessing and joy, first and foremost, because Jesus the King has fulfilled the law on our behalf and given us His righteous standing before God. This blessing and joy come to us through repentance and faith and through emulating our King, the Living Law. The culture of the kingdom, in other words, is evidenced in our lives through obedience.

Currently, the kingdom of God is the rule and reign of Jesus Christ in the hearts of those who love Him. But one day, we will take up our final *place* in the presence of our King, when we live forever with Him in the kingdom of God.

LEADER GUIDE

INTRODUCTION

Before your first meeting, encourage women to read the Introduction, watch the Session One video, and complete the personal study on pages 10–33.

GROUP SESSION ONE

Leaders, If your group members haven't watched the Session One video yet, watch it now. This week, through Old Testament prophecies foretelling the Messiah, John the Baptist setting the stage for Jesus' arrival, and descriptions of Jesus as compassionate Healer, your group members have discovered that Jesus is King and worthy of their whole lives.

ICEBREAKER QUESTION: Have you done research regarding your family tree? Did you discover any interesting facts about your lineage?

DISCUSSION QUESTIONS:

1. Why is it important for us to understand the genealogy of Jesus?
2. Jesus as King means He not only has a title, but He also holds authority. What comes to mind when you think of authority?
3. Give an example of a time when you've repented of a sin. What fruit did you see God grow in your life through repentance?
4. The Jews were looking for Jesus to reign over an earthly kingdom of shattered Roman oppressive rule, political peace, and increasing prosperity. How do you see Christians today looking for Jesus to reign in ways different than why He said He came?
5. As you recognize the promises that God keeps, how does that impact your level of trust in Him?
6. Share your takeaways from Week One with the group and close in prayer.

WATCH the Session Two video for an introduction into the coming week's study. Then remind your Bible study group to work through pages 35–61 before your next group session.

GROUP SESSION TWO

Leaders, this week we've learned how we enter the kingdom of God. We've seen the various responses Jesus received when He invited people into this kingdom. Participants have been challenged to consider how the kingdom lays claim to them.

ICEBREAKER QUESTION: What is the most unusual invitation you've ever received, and how did you respond?

DISCUSSION QUESTIONS:

1. To what types of people did Jesus extend an invitation into the kingdom? Were you surprised or confused by any of the responses Jesus received in return?
2. What has following Jesus cost you? What have you gained by following Him?
3. Describe what you learned about the Pharisees. What did they elevate? What took priority in their lives? What did they miss or resist? Were they following God?

4. What human ideas, religious traditions, or self-motivated desires do you tend to elevate over God's commandments?

5. On Day Four, the man held onto his wealth as his security and sufficiency. What are you trying to hold onto that is keeping you from loving God with all your heart? Is this giving you true life, peace, or joy? How will you respond to this awareness today?

6. In what ways have you experienced the church as a reward? In what ways has it been difficult to view the church as a reward?

WATCH the Session Three video for an introduction into the coming week's study. Then remind your Bible study group to work through pages 63–89 before your next group session.

GROUP SESSION THREE

Leaders, you and your study participants learned this week about Jesus' primary proclamation regarding the kingdom of God as He taught and ministered on earth: the culture of the kingdom.

ICEBREAKER QUESTION: What is the oddest food you put salt on?

DISCUSSION QUESTIONS:

1. How do you typically think of what the word *blessing* or *blessed* means? Look up the hashtag #blessed on social media and see how people define what it means.

2. If you named the conditions under which life would be best for you, what would you say? Would you list out the words of Jesus in Matthew 5:1-12?

3. How does Jesus define "blessed"? Who is blessed, according to Him? Which of the blessings pronounced in Matthew 5:1-12 do you struggle to see as a blessing?

4. How does knowing you *already are* the salt of the earth and the light of the world cause you to think about your life and your place in God's kingdom?

5. Do you tend to look at your own ability to "fulfill" or "accomplish" obedience or to the truth that Christ fulfilled perfect obedience and then offered that standing before God to you? If you tend to look at your own ability to obey, how does knowing that what the King has earned, you have been given?

6. How have you or those you love been affected by anger, lust, and unlawful divorce? Why were these so destructive? How does God's heart reflected in these clarified commandments bring you comfort and hope?

WATCH the Session Four video for an introduction into the coming week's study. Then remind your Bible study group to work through pages 91–113 before your next group session.

GROUP SESSION FOUR

Leaders, this week your group members have read portions of Matthew 6–7 in order to explore what it looks like to live as kingdom citizens. If we're followers of Jesus, our lives will give evidence of that through our obedience. This call to obedience is a call to spiritual health and producing spiritual fruit. It's for our joy.

ICEBREAKER QUESTION: Where are you from originally? What is a tradition or way of doing something in your family of origin that you have carried over into adulthood?

DISCUSSION QUESTIONS:

1. Have you ever done something "good" for others that wasn't motivated by a love for God or others? What were you motivated by? Did you get what you were after? What was the outcome for you?
2. When it comes to prayer, do you tend to think you have to "earn" a hearing from God by the way or length you pray? How do Jesus' words speak to your prayer life?
3. What do you think Jesus meant when He commanded us to "seek first the kingdom of God" (Matt. 6:33)?
4. What concern or worry do you need to bring under the rule and reign of Christ ("seek first the kingdom") instead of your own rule and authority (anxiety)?
5. When it comes to judgment, do you tend to consider and evaluate others more than you allow God to search and test your own heart? How do Jesus' words in Matthew 7:1-6 challenge you today?
6. Share your takeaways from Week Four with the group and close in prayer.

WATCH the Session Five video for an introduction into the coming week's study. Then remind your Bible study group to work through pages 115–139 before your next group session.

GROUP SESSION FIVE

Leaders, this week we've learned how Jesus taught and then sent His followers out to expand the kingdom of God. Readers have discovered that the kingdom's mission (and therefore their own) will not be easy. In fact, it comes with great obstacles and sometimes persecution.

ICEBREAKER QUESTION: Have you ever been given a task that felt impossible, scary, or overwhelming? What was it?

DISCUSSION QUESTIONS:

1. As Jesus was, we also are surrounded by crowds: neighbors, family members, friends, and coworkers. When you interact with people who don't know Jesus and are wandering aimlessly through life as a sheep without a shepherd, do you look at them with compassion or contempt? How does Jesus' perspective and His use of these two metaphors alter your perspective?
2. Jesus spoke to the apostles' motivation for ministering to the lost sheep of Israel. What do you think He meant when He said, "You received without paying; give without pay" (Matt. 10:8)? What had the apostles received that they were now to give?
3. When we become aware of a need or notice a lack of ministry in a certain area of the church or community, that may be an indication that God is calling us to get involved. What unmet need do

you see in your church or community that concerns you? Do you sense God "sending you out" in some way?

4. According to Jesus, what truth undergirds a lack of anxiety when we're faced with persecution or challenging situations?

5. What is an example of an unhealthy fear of man you're struggling to resist? How is this divided allegiance affecting your peace and joy? How can you replace this fear with a holy fear of God?

6. Of the gains you discovered in Day Five, Question 4, which most resonates with you? What might change in your life if you meditated consistently on your unity with Christ and what He's won you?

WATCH the Session Six video for an introduction into the coming week's study. Then remind your Bible study group to work through pages 141–165 before your next group session.

GROUP SESSION SIX

Leaders, after discovering obstacles in kingdom mission, students have studied Matthew 13 to find elements of perseverance in kingdom mission. Through Jesus' parables, He describes how the kingdom works: it's constructed slowly and often in unseen ways. As His disciples, we're cultivators in His kingdom.

ICEBREAKER QUESTION: Are you a green thumb or the opposite of a green thumb?

DISCUSSION QUESTIONS:

1. Jesus commended those who are "good soil." What makes for good soil and how is this person distinct from the ones before?

2. What cares of the world or deceitfulness of riches are choking out your desire for the Word of God? What do you need to ask God to root out in order to make your heart "good soil" for His Word?

3. In the Parable of the Talents, Jesus said that the master gave the servants different amounts of money to steward. Why was this not unfair to the servants?

4. Jesus identifies His disciples as bond-servants. Do you think of yourself as a servant who stewards what the Master owns? Or do you think of yourself as the owner of what you have and who you are? How does this perspective shape how you live?

5. In what situations or relationships are you quick to compare and envy others for what God has given them? How does this parable and John 21 speak to what you're doing? How will you respond to Jesus saying, *What does it matter? Follow me.*

6. Share your main takeaway from Week Six and then close in prayer.

WATCH the Session Seven video for an introduction into the coming week's study. Then remind your Bible study group to work through pages 167–191 before your next group session.

GROUP SESSION SEVEN

Leaders, after learning about God's role in the kingdom in Week Six, we've discovered this week that we're located in the kingdom story as a family of fellow servants. We've learned that loving others is the part we play within the kingdom over which Jesus reigns.

ICEBREAKER QUESTION: In your home growing up, what were you expected to contribute to the family?

DISCUSSION QUESTIONS:

1. Because our earthly families consist of sinful people, none of us have experienced ideal sibling relationships. But what are family relationships ideally meant to be? What does this indicate the church is meant to be?
2. How does Jesus define *greatness* in the kingdom?
3. Jesus emphasizes the private nature of approaching a brother or sister who has sinned against us. With what demeanor should we approach our brothers and sisters? With what motivation should we approach them? How are we to relate to the one who has sinned?
4. What does the distress of the watching fellow servants teach us about the consequences of unforgiveness within kingdom community?
5. Who in your life are you intentionally passing your faith onto?

WATCH the Session Eight video for an introduction into the coming week's study. Then remind your Bible study group to work through pages 193–214 before your next group session.

GROUP SESSION EIGHT

Leaders, this week readers have learned that there is a fulfillment of the kingdom still to come and how they're to live in light of this coming kingdom.

ICEBREAKER QUESTION: What was the last event or circumstance you waited expectantly for? How did you prepare for it?

DISCUSSION QUESTIONS:

1. For those who are mothers, how does Jesus' use of a labor metaphor help you understand the coming of Christ?
2. Would you say you're spending your mental energy, time, and affections on what will pass away or what will last?
3. In what ways does the delay of the coming kingdom cause you to doubt God and live for yourself? How can you cultivate a watchfulness instead?
4. How do you remember the redemption Jesus bought you? How do you keep it at the forefront of your heart and mind?
5. As we conclude our study, explain in your own words what the kingdom of God is. How do you see your place within the kingdom? And how has your perspective changed in these eight weeks of study?

Take a moment to celebrate and praise God for all He's done in and through your group during this exploration of the kingdom.

ENDNOTES

1. Patrick Schreiner, "5 Reasons Matthew Begins with a Genealogy," *The Gospel Coalition*, Jan. 1, 2020. Available online at www.thegospelcoalition.org.
2. Leon Morris, *The Gospel According to Matthew* (Grand Rapids: Wm. B. Eerdmans, 1992), 23.
3. D. A. Carson, "Matthew," in *The Expositor's Bible Commentary: Matthew, Mark, Luke,* ed. by Frank Garba (Grand Rapids: Zondervan, 1984), 74.
4. Scholars debate why Matthew chose to interchange "God" with "heaven" regarding the kingdom. For further reading, see Justin Taylor's "An Interview with Jonathan Pennington," available online at www.thegospelcoalition.org.
5. Ibid., Morris, *The Gospel According to Matthew*, 55–56.
6. Ibid., 57.
7. Ruby Buddemeyer and Charlotte Chilton, "60 Strict Rules the Royal Family Has to Follow," *Marie Claire*, Dec. 12, 2019. Available online at www.marieclaire.com.
8. ESV Study Bible (Wheaton: Crossway, 2008), 1907.
9. The phrase "doubt your doubts" comes from Tim Keller, "5 Ways to Doubt Your Doubts," *The Gospel Coalition*, Nov. 7, 2016. Available online at www.thegospelcoalition.org.
10. "*Makarios*," #3107, *Strong's Concordance*. Available online at https://biblehub.com/greek/3107.htm. Accessed on Jan. 5, 2021.
11. Ibid., Morris, *The Gospel According to Matthew*, 104.
12. Patrick Schreiner, *Matthew, Disciple and Scribe: The First Gospel and Its Portrait of Jesus* (Grand Rapids: Baker Academic, 2019), 104–109.
13. Ibid., Carson, "Matthew," 148.
14. Ibid., *The Gospel According to Matthew*, 117–118.
15. Jesus' teaching isn't intended to be used as leverage for a spiritual, physical, emotional, or sexual abuser to continue in their abuse of others. Neither are the abused called to stay under such abuse in the name of Christian forgiveness. Abuse of others is sin, and the church is to confront abusers and call upon and cooperate with civil authorities who are holding abusers accountable. For the abused, forgiveness of sins done against you doesn't necessitate restoration of relationship with an abuser.
16. Ibid., *The Gospel According to Matthew*, 137.
17. The ESV Study Bible (Wheaton: Crossway, 2008), 1833.
18. Ibid., Morris, *The Gospel According to Matthew*, 155.
19. These two paragraphs originally appeared in Christine Hoover, *With All Your Heart* (Grand Rapids: Baker, 2020), 82.
20. Greg Ogden, *Transforming Discipleship: Making Disciples a Few at a Time* (Downers Grove, IL: Intervarsity Press, 2003), 82.
21. Ibid., Carson, "Matthew," 246.
22. ESV Study Bible (Wheaton: Crossway, 2008), 1899–1900.
23. Carson, "Matthew," 316.
24. Noel Piper, *Faithful Women and Their Extraordinary God* (Wheaton, IL: Crossway, 2005), 84.
25. ESV Study Bible, 1859.
26. Ibid, Ogden, 82.
27. Aside from simply studying the Bible together, resources I recommend for use in one-on-one discipleship relationships are *Discipleship Essentials* by Greg Ogden, *Growing Together* by Melissa Kruger, *Multiply* by David Platt and Francis Chan, and *One-to-One Bible Reading* by David Helm.

HOW TO BECOME A CHRISTIAN

Jesus invites all who would come to join Him in the kingdom of God and to enjoy relationship with Him now in this life and forever with Him in eternity. If you haven't yet made the decision to follow Jesus but would like to, the Bible describes how you can do just that.

Acknowledge your sin to yourself.

We can't fully know and understand the depth and consequence of our sin, but attempting to acknowledge it as best we can is an important first step in following Jesus. Romans 3:10-12 says, "None is righteous, no, not one; no one understands; no one seeks for God. All have turned aside, together they have become worthless; no one does good, not even one." Because of our sin, we can't enter the kingdom of God and be in His presence on any merit of our own. When we recognize this, we see that we're poor in spirit—spiritually bankrupt.

Look at what Christ has done for you.

When we acknowledge we're spiritually impoverished, only then can we see the beauty of Christ's gift to us through His death and resurrection. Second Corinthians 5:21 says, "For our sake he made him to be sin who knew no sin, so that in him we might become the righteousness of God." In other words, Christ took your sin and the punishment for that sin on Himself so that He could make you right and pleasing to God and extend an invitation to you into the kingdom.

Confess your sin to God and trust in Christ for the forgiveness of your sins.

As all gifts must be accepted, the gift of Christ's work on your behalf—His invitation into the kingdom—must be received. If you want to receive the forgiveness of sins and a right relationship with God, leading to eternity in heaven with Him, confess your sin and need to God. Romans 10:9 says,

"If you confess with your mouth that Jesus is Lord and believe in your heart that God raised him from the dead, you will be saved." First John 1:9 says, "If we confess our sins, he is faithful and just to forgive us our sins and to cleanse us from all unrighteousness."

Begin to know and walk in your new identity in Christ.

Ephesians 2:4-10 says, "But God, being rich in mercy, because of the great love with which he loved us, even when we were dead in our trespasses, made us alive together with Christ—by grace you have been saved—and raised us up with him and seated us with him in the heavenly places in Christ Jesus, so that in the coming ages he might show the immeasurable riches of his grace in kindness toward us in Christ Jesus. For by grace you have been saved through faith. And this is not your own doing; it is the gift of God, not a result of works, so that no one may boast. For we are his workmanship, created in Christ Jesus for good works, which God prepared beforehand, that we should walk in them."

You are loved, approved of, made alive, joined with Christ, and created for good works. What the King has, He now shares with you.

Follow Christ.

In order to know Christ and follow Him, become a student of the Bible. When you confess your sins and trust in Christ, the Bible says that God Himself—the Holy Spirit—comes to live inside you. As you study the Bible, the Holy Spirit will help you understand what it says and obey what it says.

Finally, involve yourself in kingdom community: the church.

God uses other people to help us grow in our pursuit of Him. Join with the present kingdom—the church—in learning and cultivating the kingdom's culture.

Get the most from your study.

COMPANION PRODUCTS

Video teaching sessions, includes 8, 20–30-minute each from Christine Hoover

IN THIS STUDY, YOU'LL:

- Explore the kingdom of God in-depth, learning what the kingdom of God is and how we enter it.
- Embrace the life Jesus offers us within the kingdom and the way we find joy as His subjects.
- Understand how the ways, values, and cultivation of the kingdom of God define who we are.
- Learn to confront our allegiances to idols and false kings, re-ordering our worship.
- Identify our places in the kingdom of God and how we can join in the work that God is doing here and around the world.

To enrich your study experience, consider the accompanying *Seek First the Kingdom* video teaching sessions, approximately 20–30 minutes each, from Christine Hoover.

STUDYING ON YOUR OWN?

Watch Christine Hoover's teaching sessions, available for purchase at lifeway.com/seekfirst.

LEADING A GROUP?

Purchase the *Seek First the Kingdom - Video Streaming - Group* to show the video teaching to your group. Visit lifeway.com/seekfirst for more information on this option.

Browse companion products, a free session sample, video clips, church promotional materials, and more at

lifeway.com/seekfirst

easements 235
Ecker, O. 274
E.Coli outbreak (2013) 166
economic "booms" 45
economic choices and outcomes 217–251;
    agriculture's role in energy and climate
    change policy 246–251; conservation ethics
    and 218–219; interpreting empirical trends
    229–232; intertemporal model for analysis
    219–229; land use and soil conservation
    indicators 232–239; overview 219, 251; water
    use and 239–246
Economic Research Service (ERS): agricultural
    and environmental indicators 230, 232–239;
    agricultural productivity scenarios 267–268;
    climate change 250–251; on conservation
    230; on free trade agreements 184–185; Total
    Factor Productivity 22, 259–262
economic welfare, estimation with consumer
    and producer surplus 86–92
economies of scale 23
education: agricultural literacy 315–317;
    sustainable agriculture 266
efficiency: Agricultural Act (2014) 36–37;
    consumer and producer surplus and
    86–92; market externalities 99–101; rural
    development economics 295
Eichelsdoerfer, Petra 209
elasticities of supply-and-demand 75–76;
    demand 77–82; general principles 76–77;
    summary 85–86; supply 82–85
Electronic Benefit Transfer (EBT) 195
Emergency Assistance for Livestock, Honey
    Bees, and Farm-Raised Fish Program
    (ELAP) 128
emergency conservation programs 236
Emergency Food Security Program (EFSP) 279
empire-building 105–106, 133–134
energy, effects on agriculture and food systems
    47–55
energy crises 51
Energy Independence and Security
    Act (2007) 51
energy policy, role of agriculture in 246–248
Energy Policy Act (2005) 51
entrepreneurialism, small-scale farm
    operations 303
environment: connections to food and
    agriculture 47–50; effects on agriculture and
    food systems 47–55; and future of agricultural
    and food policy 342; interaction with
    agricultural and food policies 327–330; and
    sustainable agriculture 49–50
Environmental Protection Agency (EPA) 244
environmental quality, stocks, and flows
    measurement 230–232

Environmental Quality Incentives Program
    (EQIP) 234–235, 301, 329–330
environmental services, markets for 50
equi-marginal principle 64; in cost-benefit
    analysis 160–162; to Food Safety
    Modernization Act (FSMA) rules 160–162
equity, rural development economics 295
ethanol production 51–52, 247–248
ethics of conservation 218–219
ethnic diversity in agriculture 306–308
Eubanks, William S. 344, 346
exit option 349
expanded coverage, Crop Insurance (2014 Farm
    Bill, Title XI) 130–131
exports, currency exchange rate and 177–179;
    see also trade
extension efforts, sustainable agriculture 266
externalities see market externalities

fallacy of composition 159
Family Connections Regional Partnership 309
Farmable Wetland Program (FWP) 234
Farm Bill of 2014 see Agricultural Act of 2014
    (2014 Farm Bill)
Farmer, Michael C. 229
Farmers' Market Promotion Program (FMPP) 311
Farm Service Agency (FSA) 134, 233;
    cross-compliance 332–333
farm-to-school food programs 197, 272, 309
"Fast Track" see Trade Promotion Authority
    (TPA) ("Fast Track")
Federal Crop Insurance Corporation (FCIC) 134
Feed the Future initiative 278–279
fertilizer demand 237
Food and Nutrition Service (FNS) 194;
    administration 197; programs 195–196
Food At Home (FAH) market 81–82
Food Away From Home (FAFH) market 81–82
food deserts 281–283
food hubs 282–283, 301
food insecurity see food security and insecurity
Food Plans, role of 211–212
Food Research and Action Center (FRAC)
    207–208
food safety 342
Food Safety Modernization Act (2010) 10–11;
    cost-benefit analysis of 31–32, 152–169; cost
    incidence effects 32–33; expected economic
    effects of 30–34; goals and implementation
    30–31; influence on trade 187–188;
    performance outcomes 33–34; rules of 155,
    157–159, 167; safety by prevention policy 155
food security and insecurity 272–284; challenges
    273–274; climate change and 53; defining
    levels of 274–276; and food systems 281–282;
    local food systems and 282–283; measurement

197–198; obesity paradox 206–208; overview
274, 284; policy considerations 277–278;
private-public partnerships and 283–284;
responses to 276–281; *see also* global food
security and insecurity; nutrition programs
Food Stamp Act (1977) 195
food stamps 192, 194–195
food systems *see* agriculture and food systems
Foreign Agricultural Service (FAS) 124,
184–185
Fox, M.K. 192
fracking 246
Franklin, Benjamin 13
free riders 322
free trade 24–26, 41, 186; alongside
protectionism 185–186; factors facilitating
24; law of comparative advantage and 92–97;
politics of 25; study of agricultural 188–189
free trade agreements (FTAs) 40, 43–44,
183–185
Froman, Michael 42–43
Fuglie, Keith 266
Future Farmers of America (FFA) 317
future trends in agricultural and food policy
337–351; divergent policy agendas and
346–348; ideas on 349–350; influences
on 340–343; overview 339–340;
recommendations 348–349; transformational
vs. transitional policy change 343–346

Gaining Ground Farm (GGF) 218
Gayer, Ted 156
General Agreement on Tariffs and Trade
(GATT) 24, 180–181, 186, 326
genetic modification 315–316
Gerlt, Scott 327
Gibson, D. 207
Glauber, Joseph 131, 327
Glickman, Dan 53, 340, 342
global agricultural markets, growth of 23–25
Global Development and Environment
(GDAE) 231
global economy and US agriculture and food
sector 171–189; overview 172–173, 189;
patterns and influence 173–180; and trade
policy 180–189
Global Food Security Act (2016) 279–280,
337–339
global food security and insecurity: challenges
273–274; initiatives 278–279; trends 280
globalization 26–27; patterns and economic
influence 173–180
Global Panel on Agriculture and Food Systems
for Nutrition 325
Global Trade Analysis Project (GTAP) 13
"goodness" of policies 5
"good times" 176

Goodwin, Barry K. 36–37
Gourdji, Sharon M. 263–264
Government of Accountability Office (GAO) 333
Grandon, Eric 301
Great Depression 23, 37, 45, 50, 182, 194
Great Recession 45–46, 192–193
"green box" category 182, 327
greenhouse gas (GHG) emissions 53–54, 239
Gross Domestic Product (GDP): relations to
imports 176–177; and rural areas 22
groundwater use 242–243
Gunderson, Craig 276–278

Haskins, Ron 208
Headey, D.D. 274
Health and Human Services (HHS) 192–193;
Administration for Community Living
(HHS-ACL) 196–197; dietary guidelines
207–208
Healthy Eating Index 192
Hicks-Kaldor criterion 168
Hierarchy of Needs 26
High Food Security 275
Hirschman, Albert 349–350
Hite, James C. 290–291
Hodge, Ian 289, 294–295
Honadle, Beth Walter 292–293
household consumer choice, analysis of
199–201
household consumers: agricultural literacy of
315–317; in-kind transfer programs 202–204;
intertemporal model 221–227; nutritional
recommendations for 212–213
household food security 275–278, 280–281; local
food system innovation for 282–284
hunger 197–198, 275

immigrants in agriculture 301
imports, in relation to Gross Domestic Product
176–177
Impossibility Theorem 105
income distribution 168, 186–189
incremental policy improvements 344–345
Indifference Curve 200–201
infra-marginal case 204–205
infrastructure investment, sustainable agriculture
266–267
in-kind transfer programs 198–204
integrated rural development model (IRPM)
(World Bank) 295–296
Internal Rate of Return (IRR) 165
International Food Security Assessment (IFSA)
280–281
international trade *see* trade
Internet of Things 333
intertemporal choice model 219–229; analysis
219–221, 227; assumptions and basic

framework 221–223; and challenges of
sustainable development 227–229; external
cost (scenario one) 223–224; internalized
external cost (scenario two) 224–226; market
distortions and household decisions 223; and
resource allocation 230–232
Iron Triangle theory 106; and crop insurance
132–134, 145
irreversible change in land use 219
irrigation efficiency 237

Jablonski, B.B.R. 283
Janssen, L. 329
job creation, as benefit and/or cost 159–160
Joerger, R.M. 266

Kay, D. 283
Keeney, Roman 325–326
Kennedy, E.T. 192
"Know Your Farmer, Know Your Food" initiative
311–312
Knutson, Ronald D. 32, 34
Kramer-LeBlanc, C.S. 192
Krautkraemer, Jeffrey A. 227
Kreider, Brent 276–278
Krutilla, John 220–221

labor costs, unemployment effects on 156
land retirement programs 233–234
land use and soil conservation indicators
232–239; program participation 233–236
Law of Comparative Advantage 24–25, 92–93,
173, 186; and economic realities 96–97; and
opportunity cost principle 93; US-Mexico
trade (scenario) 93–96
Law of Demand 68
Law of Supply 67
Liberal Food Plan 211–212
Lichtenberg, Eric 328–329
Lincoln, Abraham 1–2
Livestock Forage Disaster Program (LFP) 128
Livestock Indemnity Program (LIP) 128
Loan Deficiency Payments (LDPs) 118
Lobell, David B. 263–264
Local Food Marketing Promotion Program
(LFPP) 311
local food markets, expanding role of 309–311
local food systems 282; definition difficulties
310; food insecurity challenges 273–274;
innovation 282–283; organic production
and 312; policy effects on development
310–311
localized agriculture, and rural development
policy 296
local leadership, sustainable food-secure
solutions 283–284
logic of collective action 341–342, 350

Low-Cost Food Plans 211–212
Low Food Security 275
Lubben, B. 329–330
Lucas, Frank 323–324

Mabli, J. 192
MacDonald, James 28
McDonald's 27
macroeconomics: counter-cyclical policy
("Great Recession" scenario) 45–46; currency
exchange rate and trade 46–47, 176–179;
impact of nutrition programs 192; impacts of
fiscal and monetary policies 44–45; influences
on agriculture and food systems 44–47
Malthus, Thomas 220–221
marginal analysis 64; of Minnesota farmland-
waterway buffer-strip (scenario) 64–66
marginal rate of substitution 200
market analysis *see* supply-and-demand model
(S&D Model)
market distortions: Agricultural Act (2014)
118–119, 122; and intertemporal household
decisions 223, 227
market equilibrium: analysis 70–71; example
scenarios 72–75
market externalities 97; economic efficiency
impact analysis 99–101; market failure 97;
origins, challenges and alternatives 97–98;
scenario 98–99; side effects of successful air
pollution control programs 101; and water
quality 243–244
market failure 97–98
marketing, organic production and 312–313
Marketing Assistance Loan Program (MALP;
2014 Farm Bill, Title I - Subtitle B) 118–119
market price determination 69–70; market
equilibrium analysis 70–75
market shortage analysis 70
market surplus analysis 70
Marshall, Alfred 66
Masters, Will 331
maximum attainable profit level 64
maximum total satisfaction 63
Maxwell, Simon 296–297
Mayer, Igor 5, 8
measurable program benefit 118
Mickey Leland Memorial Domestic Hunger
Relief Act (1990) 195
microeconomics: currency exchange rate
and trade 177–179; perspective on rural
developments 294–295; *see also* intertemporal
choice model
Midmore, Peter 289, 294–295
Milk Income Loss Contract Program (MILC)
121–122, 132, 144, 187–188
Millennium Development Goals (UN)
275, 280

Minnesota Farm Business Management
    Education program 266
Minnestota farmland-waterway buffer-strip
    (scenario) 64–65
minority farm operators: characteristics and
    contributions of 306–308; opportunities and
    incentives for 308–309
mitigation of climate change effects 54
Moderate-Cost Food Plans 211–212
Moon, Wanki 185
"Most Favored Nation" status 181
multi-dimensional consumers 28
multilateralism, trade policy 180–186
multiplier effect 159
Munisamy, Gopinath 267
MyPlate *vs.* MyPyramid, nutritional
    recommendations 212–213

National Agricultural Literacy Outcomes
    316–317
National Agricultural Statistics Service (NASS)
    129, 230
national business cycle 45
National Oceanic and Atmosphere
    Administration (NOAA) 248
National Organic Program (NOP) 313
National Research Council (NRC) 197–198
national treatment principle
    (trade agreements) 181
natural resources: interaction with agricultural
    and food policies 327–330; quality *vs.*
    quantity 220; *see also* conservation;
    environment
Natural Resources Conservation Service
    (NRCS) 218, 230, 232–233; cross-compliance
    332–333; opportunities for socially
    disadvantaged groups 308
Naylor, Rosamond 274–275, 295–296, 324
Ndagijimana, Janine 301
negotiating rounds (WTO) 181–182
Nelson, Rebecca 264
Net Present Value (NPV) 163–166
Neumayer, Eric 229
New Rural Paradigm 292–293
Nigeria, rural development and palm oil
    production (case study) 290–292
Niskanen, William 106
non-point water pollution 244–245
North American Free Trade Agreement
    (NAFTA) 12, 25, 182–183, 186–187
nutritional recommendations, MyPyramid *vs.*
    MyPlate 212–213
nutrition programs 191–214; coordination
    with agricultural policies 330–331; effects
    of 204–205; evaluating impacts of 197–198;
    food safety nets 192–193; in-kind transfer
    programs 198–204; obesity *vs.* food insecurity

paradox 206–208; overview 193, 213–214;
    recommendations to household consumers
    212–213; review of 194–197; role of Food
    Plans 211–212; Thrifty Food Plan 208–211

Obama, Barack 279–280, 338
Obama Administration: local food system
    development 311; Waters of the United
    States (WOTUS) 244–245
Oberholtzer, Lydia 312–313
obesity 206–208, 281
Ogallala Aquifer 242
O'Hara, Sabine 283
Ohls, M.K. 192
Okrent, A.M. 331
Olson, Mancur 321–322, 333, 350
Omnibus Trade and Competitiveness Act
    (1988) 183
opportunity cost 63–64
optimization 63–64
option demand concept 220
Orden, David 47
Organic Foods Production Act (1990) 313
organic production: certification, *vs.* alternative
    farm systems 313–314; and local food systems
    312; marketing 312–313
Organization for Economic Cooperation and
    Development (OECD): agricultural and
    environmental indicators 230, 237–239;
    Green Growth initiative 263; on rural
    development 292–293; on total factor
    productivity 259–260
Outreach and Assistance to Socially
    Disadvantaged Farmer and Rancher Program
    (SDFR) 308–309

palm oil production in Nigeria (case study)
    290–292
Pareto, Vilfredo 91–92
Pareto-Better transactions 91–92
Parke, Wilde 205
paternalistic approach 204
Pease, J. 329–330
Pepper, John 276–278
pesticide use 237
Peterson Institute for International
    Economics 43
Petri, Peter 41
Pezzy, John C.V. 229
planned policy change 345
Plummer, Michael 41
policy analysis 1–17; challenges and efficacy of
    4–5; influential 10–13; overview 2–5, 14–17;
    and policymaking 2; systematic method for
    (steps 1-6) 7–8; textbook guidelines 14
policy analysis toolbox 5–9, 60–107; comparative
    advantage 92–97; conclusions 107;

consumer and producer surplus, using 86–92; demand-and-supply elasticities 75–86; market externalities and public goods 97–103; overview 62–63; positive economic analysis 63–66; public choice economics 103–107; supply and demand 66–75
policy design, science and art of 8–9
policy evaluation 5–9
policymaking 2
political economy of crop insurance 131–132
population trends 20
positive economic analysis 63–65; Minnesota farmland-waterway buffer-strip (scenario) 64–65
poverty and food insecurity 276–277
poverty reduction, and rural development 296–297
precipitation patterns 242
precision agriculture methods 262
premium subsidies, crop insurance 130–131
present value (PV) 163
preventative model 49
price elasticity of demand 77–79
price elasticity of supply 82–85; US wheat market-price volatility (scenario) 84–85
Price-Loss Coverage Program (PLC) 113–117, 327
producer surplus *see* consumer and producer surplus
product development, crop insurance 130–131
productivity *see* agricultural productivity
property rights 225
protectionism 23, 25–26, 40, 44; law of comparative advantage and 92–97; trade policy and 180–186
public choice economics 103–107; and Agricultural Act (2014) 146–147; and alternative voter preferences 104; definition and contribution to policy analysis 103–104; future and 107; impossible outcomes and rational choice calculus 105; Iron Triangle 106; rent-seeking and empire-building 105–106
public good 97, 101–103; benefits 322; Food Safety Modernization Act and 158–159; outcomes, research and development 265
public–private partnerships, sustainable food-secure solutions 283–284
public water projects 243

quantitative easing 46
quasi-fixed asset modifications 264

Randall, Alan 227, 229
Ranney, Christine 205
rational consumer choice theory 199
rationality 63–64
Ray, Daryll E. 27
recession *see* Great Recession

Reciprocal Trade Agreements Act (1934) 23
Regional Conservation Partnership Program (RCPP) 235
regional free trade agreements 183–184
regionalism and trade policy 180–186
regional partnerships, soil conservation programs 235–236
Regulatory Impact Analysis (RIA) 158, 160
regulatory systems 48
remedial policy change 345
renewable energy 52–53, 246–248
Renewable Energy for America Program (REAP) 248
Renewable Fuel Standard (RFS) 51
rent seeking 105–106, 133
research and development (R&D) 22, 53–54; sustainable agriculture 265–268
Resilience program 283
Ribaudo, M. 328
Ribera, Luis A. 32, 34
Ricardo, David 93–94
Rickard, B.J. 331
risk aversion 167–168
Risk Management Agency (RMA) 129–131, 134
risk premium 167
Robertson, Richard 48–49
Robinette, Beth 301
Roe, Terry L. 267
Rogers, Robert 164
Roosevelt, Franklin D. 182–183
Rose, Donald 209
Rosen, Harvey 107, 156
rural development 287–297; anticipating policy challenges and opportunities 294–297; business succession and 287–288; evolving role of agriculture in 289–290; introduction 288–289; need for comprehensive approaches to 290; overview 289, 297; palm oil production in Nigeria (case study) 290–292; patterns in 293–294; proposals to modernize policies on 292–293

Sackett, Hillary 314
Safe Minimum Standards (SMS), decision-making method 229
Saldias, Gabriel 185
Samuelson, Paul 4
Saxowsky, David M. 26
scarcity 63–64
Schaffer, Harwood D. 27
Schmit, T.M. 283
school meal programs 193, 207
Schuh, G. Edward 47
Schultz, Theodore W. 296
secondary effects 159
self-interest 63
Senauer, Ben 26, 205

Senegal, National Biogas Program 272
sensitivity analysis 164–165
shadow prices, estimating 156
shallow-loss program 129–130
Shumway, C. Richard 264
Shupp, Robert 314
Simpson, R. David 230
Slack, Tim 192–193
slippage 329
small-scale farm operations: vs. large-scale
    302–303; socioeconomics and market entry
    for 304; strengths and limitations of 303–304
Smith, Adam 93, 346
Smith, Vincent H. 36–37
Smoot-Hawley Tariff Act (1930) 23–25, 111
socially disadvantaged groups in agriculture 301;
    characteristics and contributions of 306–308;
    opportunities and incentives for 308–309
soil conservation 233–236; easements 235;
    indicators 232–239; land retirement programs
    233–234; regional partnerships 235–236;
    working lands programs 234–235
soil erosion 232–233
soy-based biodiesel 247
Specter, S.E. 206–207
spillover effects 48
Spokane, Washington 301
Stabenow, Debbie 132–133
Stacked Income Protection Plan (STAX)
    129–130
Standard Reinsurance Agreement (SRA) 134
State of Food Insecurity in the World report 280
stocks and flows, agricultural and environmental
    230–232
strong sustainability 228; vs. weak 228–229
sugar program see US Sugar Program (2014 Farm
    Bill, Title I - Subtitle C)
Sullivan, Kate 315
Summer Food Service Program 192
Summit on Global Development, US White
    House 337–338
Supplemental Agricultural Disaster Assistance
    Programs (2014 Farm Bill, Title I - Subtitle E)
    127–128
Supplemental Coverage Option (SCO) 116,
    130–131
Supplemental Nutrition Assistance Program
    (SNAP) 192–198; consumer analysis 202–204;
    food insecurity and 278; food security
    initiatives 284; interpretation of evidence for
    204–205; nutritional guidelines for 212–213;
    relationship with food insecurity and obesity
    207–208; and the Thrifty Food Plan 209–210
Supplemental Revenue Assistance (SURE) crop
    disaster program 127, 132
supply-and-demand model (S&D Model) 66;
    changing market equilibria 72–75; demand

function 68–69; foundations and organization
    of 66; market price determination 69–71;
    supply function 67–68; see also elasticities of
    supply-and-demand
supply function 67–68
surface water supply 243
sustainability 256–269, 314; alternative
    scenarios and policy options 264–268;
    economic forces for change 258–262; future
    of 268–269, 283–284, 342, 348; integration
    of productivity and climate change 262–264;
    intertemporal choice and challenges of
    227–229; meaning and purpose of 314–315;
    overview 257–258, 268–269; policy
    interaction 328; profitable systems integration
    49–50; strong and weak 228–229
Sustainable Agriculture Research and Education
    Program (SARE) 315

Takoma Park, Maryland 301
Tanentzap, Andrew J. 328
Tariff Rate Quotas (TRQs) 13, 121, 124,
    140–144, 188
tariffs 188
taxation, distributional effects and real costs 157
technical assistance conservation programs 236
technical efficiency gains 261
technological advancement 261
technological treadmill 259
technology in agriculture 237; and future policy
    340–341; productivity and 22–23
Technology Transfer Act (1986) 265–266
Temporary Assistance for Needy Families
    (TANF) 193
Thrifty Food Plan (TFP) 208–211; importance
    of 208–209; perspectives on 209–210;
    political considerations 210–211
Tilman, David 262
Toman, Michael A. 229–230
Tonsor, Glynn 314
tools for policy analysis see policy analysis toolbox
Tornqvist Index-Estimation Methodology 258
Total Factor Productivity (TFP) 22, 259–262
Total Maximum Daily Load (TMDL), water
    pollutants 244
trade: consumer and producer surplus
    (scenario) 88–91; contribution of US
    agriculture to 175–176; and future of
    agricultural and food policy 341; historical
    and political perspective 182–183; influence
    of macroeconomic policy and exchange
    rates 46–47; law of comparative advantage
    and 92–97; political developments 25–29;
    US WTO commitments and 2014 Farm Bill
    325–327; see also free trade; protectionism;
    Trans-Pacific Partnership (TPP)
Trade Act (2015) 12–13, 38

trade adjustment assistance 96
trade creation 43, 184
trade dispute resolution 181
trade diversion 43, 184
trade liberalization *see* free trade
trade-offs 127
Trade Openness Ratio 174
Trade Promotion Authority (TPA) ("Fast Track")
    12–13, 183
trade war 23, 25
Trans-Atlantic Trade and Investment
    Partnership (TTIP) 25, 183
transformational policy change 343–344
transitional policy change 345
Trans-Pacific Partnership (TPP) 12–13, 25, 144,
    183, 188; costs, benefits, and distributional
    effects 40–42; economic modeling of
    influence 41–42; expected economic effects
    38–44; expected performance outcomes
    42–44; goals and implementation 39–40;
    US participation and ethanol import tariffs
    (scenario) 88–91
transparency (trade agreements) 181, 182,
    187, 348
Tree Assistance Program (TAP) 128
trickle-down effect 159
Tristan (example consumer) 167
Truman, Harry 343
Trump, Donald J. 40
Tullock, Gordon 104–105, 146
Turner, R. Kerry 228–229
Tyndall, John 229

uncertainty, decision making under 166–168
unemployment effects on labor costs 156
United Nations (UN), *Sustainable Development
    Solutions Network* 263
United Nations Food and Agriculture
    Organization (FAO) 290
United Nations Framework Convention on
    Climate Change (UNFCCC) 53
United States Geological Survey (USGS) 240
Uruguay Round Agreement on Agriculture
    (URAA) 327
"Uruguay Round of Talks" (GATT) 173, 180,
    182–183
US Congressional Research Service (CRS) 113
US Dairy Program (2014 Farm Bill, Title I -
    Subtitle D) 121–127; changes and trade
    impacts 42, 122–123; impacts summary
    126–127; new DMPP and DPDP dairy
    programs 122–123; policy considerations
    influencing markets 123–126
US Federal Reserve Bank, monetary policy
    and 45
US Sugar Program (2014 Farm Bill, Title I -
    Subtitle C) 42, 44, 119–121

value chain, vertical coordination in 27–28
$Value of Sales by Commodity Group
    ($VSGC) 306
Van Daalen, Els 5, 8
vertical coordination in the value chain 27–28
Very Low Food Security 275–276
Veterans and Warriors Agriculture Program
    (VW) 301
veterans in agriculture 301, 309
Vilsack, Tom 192, 256–257
voice option 349–350
vote-maximization 132–133

Walmart 27, 342
Ward, William A. 290–291
water demand 240–241
water pollution, non-point 244–245
Water Pollution Control Act (1972)
    ("Clean Water Act") 244–245
water quality, market externalities and
    243–244
watershed conservation programs 236
Waters of the United States (WOTUS)
    interpretative rule 244–245
water supply 241–243
water use: and the agri-food system 239–243;
    economic influences on 239–246; irrigation
    237, 241–242
weak sustainability 228; *vs.* strong 228–229
weighted-value indices of agricultural outputs
    and inputs 258
Westhoff, Patrick 327
Wetland Reserve Easements 235
Wholesome Wave Fruit and Vegetable
    Prescription Program (FVRx) 284
Women, Infant and Children Program (WIC)
    193, 195–197
women farm operators 301; characteristics
    and contributions of 304–305; commodities
    marketed by 306
Working Lands Programs 234–235
World Bank, on rural development 295–296
World Commission on Environment and
    Development (WCED) 227
World Trade Organization (WTO) 144;
    Agreement on Agriculture (AoA) 122–123,
    182–188; influence on international trade
    180–181, 186; and Law of Comparative
    Advantage (LCA) 96; rules and agricultural
    markets 182; trade principles 181; US trade
    commitments and 2014 Farm Bill 325–327

Yang, Sansi 264
You, Wen 209
Young, Nathan 205

Zhai, Fan 41